365-DAY SOUL WINNING QUEST

Matthew 28:19-20 "Go therefore and make disciples of all the nations, baptizing them in the name of the Father and of the Son and of the Holy Spirit, teaching them to observe all things that I have commanded you; and lo, I am with you always, *even* to the end of the age." Amen

Chancellor Searcy

ISBN: 1500684279
ISBN 13: 9781500684273

TABLE OF CONTENTS

ACKNOWLEDGMENTS

I would first and foremost like to give honor to my Lord and savior Jesus Christ who is the head of my life. I would like to thank my wife, Nicole, for being in my corner through everything that I've been through with this quest, and also inspiring, uplifting, and encouraging me whenever I felt like quitting. Iron truly does sharpen iron. (**Pro. 27:17**) I want to thank my mother, Marion, for bringing in me into this world. Without my mother, there would be no me. I would also like to thank my spiritual leaders, Pastor Reginald & Delphine Glenn, for under girding and spiritually strengthening me. They are the shepherds of Judah Evangelistic Ministries. I further want to acknowledge and thank my brother in Christ, Minister Dorian Harvey, who is also a member of my church. You will hear his name a lot throughout this book. He is one of my most faithful soul winning partners. Lastly, I want to thank all the members of my church who were constantly praying for me and interceding on my behalf. Prayer is the best and most powerful support.

INTRODUCTION

My name is Chancellor Searcy and I am married to my beautiful wife, Nicole. I am a proud member of Judah Evangelistic Ministries. My church is a very powerful and much anointed church. I am the leader of our Soul Winning Witnessing team. I am also a member of IYM (Incarcerated Youth Ministry), a youth ministry that allows me to minister to incarcerated youths. I have served 6 years in the United States Army National Guard. I am currently a Detroit Police Officer. I have been saved since 2008. In the year of 2012, I set a quest to minister to a different person every day of the year. I ministered close to 800 different people in that year. I encountered a lot of special people during my quest and had some miraculous things take place. I have documented every encounter with everyone that I witnessed on each day of 2012. I am writing this book unto God in hopes that it will inspire people to evangelize more. I have allowed the Holy Spirit to inspire and guide me through this book. Although every person that I encountered throughout the year was significant and important, I only wrote about the most significant encounters that I feel would have an impact on witnessing. I know that there are many people that will be skeptical and not believe all the things in this book, but a false testimony is not a testimony at all. I have kept and stored away all of my documents in relation to this quest. God doesn't receive any praise if I lie in His name. I am writing this book to strengthen believers in their daily walk with Christ and to help strengthen, empower, and encourage them in the area of evangelism. I am also writing this book to the lost and unsaved in hopes that the things written in this book will persuade you to open up your heart to truth and begin to serve a true and living God. I want everyone to understand that no matter what your title is, whether it be a Minister, Pastor, Apostle, Elder, Bishop, etc., you are not exempt from evangelizing or spreading the word of God. I just pray that whoever reads this book will be encouraged, begin to evangelize more, and reach out to the lost and sinful. **"I have come not to bring the righteous, but the sinners into repentance" -Luke 5:32.**

1

MY LIFE & GROWTH

I grew up in a household where my mom was saved and whenever we went to church, it's because we were forced to go. When my mom started working on Sundays, we stopped going to church. I used to stay in my room by myself many times and read the bible to try to get an understanding on it, and on 'life'. Though without church, it was hard to understand the scriptures. As I grew older and became an adult, like a lot of other children, I began wanting to experience life. I began drinking and clubbing and doing other sinful things. I got saved in September 2008. I remember visiting Judah Evangelistic Ministries with my now wife, Nicole, who I had just met a couple of months before then. She had been a member since the inception of the ministry. I remembered that day in great detail. When I walked into the church it was during intermission time and everyone began to greet me and was so friendly and genuinely nice toward me. During praise and worship, I just stood there because I didn't know or understand what was going on. I had never been to a church that praised and worshipped. I was used to hearing choir songs and everyone singing together in unity. Pastor Reggie (Reginald) preached a good sermon about being saved, living a holy lifestyle, and going to Heaven or Hell. After his sermon, Pastor Reggie called me up to pray for me. I remember him anointing me with oil and laying his hands on my head and telling me things about my life that he couldn't have known. He prophesied over my life and told me that God was calling me to be saved. I have never had anyone lay hands on me or speak anything over my life prophetically. Right then and there I gave my life to God. I didn't know what it took to be saved or to make it to Heaven, but I knew that I did not want to go to Hell. From that moment on, I began to live for God and never went back to the world again. I called my best friend, Quincy, and told him that I got saved and that I couldn't do the same things that we used to do. I put everything behind me. I began to read the bible and study scriptures every day. Other men in the church would call me to check up on me and encourage me. It also felt good having pastors that I could call and converse with and also get enlightenment from. I called Pastor Dell (Delphine) a lot with questions and concerns that I had. I am thankful that she always had the right answer for me and was able to uplift me. It was also most certainly good to have Nicole by my side to help me live holy and keep me from slipping whenever I even thought about it.

At that time I was driving a little car, working as a door-to-door salesman contracted through AT&T selling Uverse cable, and living at home with my mother. I wasn't where I wanted to be in my life; but I was newly saved and on fire for God. God began to move in my life. I moved to Indiana for better a job opportunity within my company and used to drive back and forth every other week to see Nicole, my family, and most importantly to attend church. It was about a five hour drive. One Sunday afternoon in late October while I was driving back to Indiana for work, the Detroit Police Department (DPD) called me to come in and start work for them the following day. This was ironic and definitely a blessing from God seeing that I hadn't heard from DPD in over 1 ½ years since I first started the background process. So, I turned around and headed back to Detroit; and that's when everything had started to go uphill for me. I had set an appointment to go through a deliverance at Judah one Sunday afternoon in November of that same year. The purpose of the deliverance was to remove a lot of anger that I had stored up inside of me. I really didn't know these people, but like I said earlier I just wanted to be saved and set free from any evil that was within me. It was nothing to be ashamed of. Many people look at deliverances as a weakness, but it is really just another part of submitting to God and relinquishing all power to Him and restoring your spirit. **"If we confess our sins, he is faithful and just to forgive us [our] sins, and to cleanse us from all unrighteousness" -1 John 1:9.** I had drill with the Army National Guard that whole weekend. I had woken up at 5:00 am and had been at drill all day since that time. I remembered leaving drill around 6:00 pm and still being in my Army uniform. I called Pastor Reggie and told him that I was on my way. He told me that I could reschedule if I wanted to. I told him that I wanted to be fully set free and renewed and that I was on my way. When I got there, we got straight to it. Pastor Reggie and Pastor Dell were there with several other ministers from Judah. Pastor Reggie laid hands on me, and he along with the other ministers began to pray for me. Shortly after, I joined in with the praying. After about 5 minutes of praying, I had received the Holy Spirit and began speaking in tongues. I will never forget it. It felt like there was nothing else around me. All I saw was a bright light and I couldn't move. This was probably the most amazing experience that I have ever encountered in my life.

From that day forth, I began to minister to people about God's love and mercy. I didn't care who was around or where I was, I would minister about Jesus. My family noticed a difference in me and my attitude, but was still skeptical of course. Your family and closest friends are usually the hardest people to minister to. This is because they knew you when you were a sinner and are doubtful of your new lifestyle and change. I've learned through my experience, that just continuing to live a holy righteous lifestyle will draw them closer to believing in the 'new you'. I remember some of my family members came up to Michigan from Georgia to visit us. They looked at me, the way I spoke, the way I moved, and my conversation, which was all about God and just knew that I was different. I remember one of my uncles making a comment about me saying, "he's just on fire now, it will go away after a while". I said to myself, "If he only knew". I thought about the scripture (**Jeremiah 20:9**) -*His word* **was in my heart as a burning fire shut up in my bones**. Here this older man was who had been in church his whole life and had allowed his fire to burn out. The fire that I have for God is on the inside and will forever burn to be released. That was when I first began to work on being rejected. At that time, I hadn't really encountered anyone that rejected the gospel of Jesus or had different beliefs than me, but that confrontation forced me to prepare for the inevitable. So, I began to read my word more and more to prepare for rejection while being out ministering the gospel of Jesus to others. The bible tells us to always be ready to defend our faith. (**1 Peter 3:15**)

During my time in the Detroit Police Academy, I endured a lot of scoffing. I was a "loner" and stayed to myself most of the time. Most of my classmates didn't want to hear about Jesus and I didn't want to hear about sin. It was kind of tough though because the whole concept of the Academy was to be unitized. I didn't like the dirty jokes, childish games, or the weekend drinking, etc. I was also ostracized a lot. When you are a child of God, you will bring light to darkness and find a way to shine through it. The bible says that we are the light of the world. (**Matthew 5:14**) I just want anyone who is reading this book that is facing; bullying, rejection from peers/parents, isolation, or even loneliness, to know that once you come into Christ, you become part of **"a chosen generation", "a royal priesthood", "a holy nation", and "a peculiar people"**. (**1 Peter 2:9**) Please stay encouraged, it is not the end of the world. God loves you, so find joy in him. Think about it, once you get saved, you become the adopted child of the Creator. Who is more powerful than Him, and now He is your father and you are in His hands of protection. **"If God is for you, who can be against** you"- **Romans 8:31.** People spat on Jesus, whipped Him severely, beat Him beyond recognition, and even killed Him, but he stayed humble and forgiving. The bible tells us that in well doing you will put to silence the ignorance of foolish people. **(1 Peter 2:15)** This scripture is what kept me humble and helped me make it through all that I endured during the academy process. Also God tells us that he will deal with our enemies and scoffers. **(Romans 15:3)** Overall, I had a great time in the Police Academy, gained a lot of knowledge, and made some great friends after it was all said and done. In spite of everything I went through, I never compromised my holiness. **Always stand firm on your holiness, let no one cause you to sin.**

In June 2009, I proposed to Nicole and she gracefully accepted. In December 2009, I moved out of my mother's house and into my first apartment. I was overly excited to have my own living space. This meant that I could now pray as loud as I wanted to. In June 2010, I married Nicole and moved into a bigger and better apartment. At that time, I still had not encountered any real rejection dealing with another religion while ministering to people. In January 2011, Pastor Reggie appointed me leader over Judah's witnessing team. It was a team that went out at least once a month to wherever God led us, and we spread the word of Jesus to people. I named the team 'Soul Redeemers', and we went into effect around June 2011. For the most part, it was Dorian and I hitting the streets on Saturday, but other church member joined when they were available. One Saturday, Dorian and I were at Fairlane Mall witnessing when I finally encountered someone who rejected the gospel of Jesus. We met a Muslim who was strong in his faith. I thank God for Dorian who has a lot of knowledge of other religions and practices. He was able to dialogue with the guy about the Quran while I told him about Jesus. In the end, he became aggressive, didn't want to hear it, and walked away. The man was not responsive, but it was still a learning experience for me. God is so omniscient and wise in allowing things to happen in his timing. The one time I faced rejection, I had someone to back me up who had knowledge in that area. I had finally known what it felt like to have the gospel of Jesus rejected. That one day was just the beginning of a lot more to come.

2

GETTING STARTED

The whole year of 2011, I had been praying for more bold-ness to minister to people and for God to send people my way that needed to hear about Jesus. It seemed like that one Saturday at Fairlane mall triggered the Devil. I began to deal with all kinds of rejection. People would just ignore me whenever I tried to minister to them, but I learned to overcome. I had a lot of knowledge of God's word, but it wasn't enough for me. I wanted to know and understand why people chose their faith and their re-ligion, so I began to read about other religions. A lot of the knowl-edge that I gained was through actual experiences and encounters with people of different religions who would explain their religion to me. It seemed for every religion that I stumbled across, different people of the same religion had different thoughts or practices for that religion. And, it seemed that Christianity was the only religion that was the same across the board. I want people to know that before you start learning about other religions or different types of faith, be strong in your own faith. I was able to draw people into the word of God just by dialoging with them about Jesus and trying to figure out why they chose the faith that they did. These encounters strengthened me. They improved me. So although I was a 'babe in Christ' (which means that I was newly saved), I was rapidly maturing in the things of God. But I still wanted more. I had a strong heart for God's people and wanted to save everybody.

One night in late November, I went into prayer and I began to ask God for more boldness. Although I would minister to people all the time, I was still hesitant to minister to certain individuals and would pass up a lot of people. I prayed for more sensitivity to the Spirit to know who to minister to. I began to weep, and weep, and weep, and cry out to the Lord. Then I got silent. Sometimes you have to get silent before the Lord. We bombard Him with all of our problems and complaints. While we're busy complaining, He's telling us how to fix it, but we can't hear Him because we are busy talking. So sometimes you have to just lay before God and just soak in His presence and don't get up until he releases you to. Also stop crying over spilled milk, when most of the time God is the one that spilled it. So while I was sitting there silent, the Lord spoke to me. I heard him speak to me very clearly. He told me, "If you want to be **BOLD**, be **BOLD**". He then put it in my spirit to begin to witness to someone every day. Judah was set to have a 'Watchnight Service', which is when you spend New Year's Eve inside the church bringing in the New Year praising and worshipping God. I was unable to make the service because I had to work. The night before I had prayed, and while I was in prayer I was thinking of a way to take my holiness to a new level for the New Year. While the world makes "new year resolutions", Christians make "new year dedications". So while in prayer, the Lord told me again, "If you want to be **BOLD**, be **BOLD**". I told Nicole to let the church know at Watchnight service that my dedication to the Lord for the New Year was to minister to a different person every day of the year for 2012. Once I told her that, I didn't know how I was going to do it, but I knew that it was a vow to God and that I had to carry it out. I began to pray and ask God for strength, guidance, and wisdom.

The Lord soon revealed to me how to complete this task. He told me to use Microsoft Excel to document everything. He told me how to document everything and exactly what to document. I documented the date I ministered to the person, the time, the person's name, where I was when I ministered to them, what we talked about, whether they received salvation or not, if they were going to visit my church, and their phone number. I knew that I had a difficult task ahead of me. Pastor Reggie told me that he didn't know anyone else in his whole lifetime that had ever set forth a goal similar to mine. The members of the church had faith in me and were confident that I would complete it. I was nervous and didn't even know where to start or who to minister to first. I was confused as to what I should do if I didn't see anyone for a whole day. So I began to pray, pray, and pray for peace and tranquility. Then out of nowhere, I felt peace like nothing else in the world mattered (**Philippians 4:7**). I felt confident and ready to take on the task.

3

JANUARY

S
o here we go! It was the first day of the year and I was excited to tell somebody about Jesus. The whole day Nicole and I had visited different family member's houses to celebrate the New Year. I saw many people. I saw saved people. I saw unsaved people. Most of the day went by and I hadn't witnessed to anyone. I had got hurt at work in late 2011 and was still working the front desk at my precinct on restricted duty. I wasn't seriously hurt, I had just twisted my ankle. I had to be at work at 11:00 pm that night. I went to work and was sitting at the desk thinking to myself, "What am I going to do? The year just started and I'm about to fail already." As police officers we are discouraged to talk about religion or politics while at work. At 11:45 pm, a fellow officer walked up to me and began to talk to me about the New Year and I began to minister to him. He told me that he was waiting till the time was right to give his life to God. Of course I mentioned to him the story of Noah's Ark. I also told him that life isn't promised and that we are here for a little while and then we're gone. (**James 4:14**) He stuck with his current disposition. You have to understand and realize that not everyone is going to receive your word, no matter how you minister it to them. It can be bold or passive. Some people just like the way they are living and are content with their lifestyle. Sometimes all you can do is plant the seed (word of God). Someone else will come through and water your seed. You

are just the Planter, who plants the seed, but not the Gardener who waters the seed. Neither the one who plants nor the one who waters is anything, but it is only God that gives the increase and makes things grow. **(1 Corinthians 3:7)** So don't be discouraged. That person will have to give an account on why they continued in the error of their ways after hearing the Word of God. After ministering to him, I felt relieved and happy. I was disappointed at myself for waiting so long to minister to someone, but I also was excited and felt 'in the groove'.

So, day one was over and I was determined from that day on to not delay in witnessing to someone. That same shift at work, I ministered to another fellow officer named Charles Lynem. He is a really good guy and a great police officer, and currently my partner. It is ironic because when I tried to minister to him, we weren't partners and he was kind of standoffish and told me that he didn't believe in the whole bible. Now with us being partners, I have had many opportunities to minister to him and he is in the process of growing closer to God. On January 4th, I went to a store called Meijer, and encountered two young guys working there named Kevin and John. One of the guys told me that he had a really bad attitude and the other guy said that he was saved but hadn't been filled with the Holy Spirit. Being filled with the power of the Holy Spirit is a vital part of your walk with God. After receiving salvation, it is imperative that you seek to be filled with the Holy Spirit. The bible says, **"you shall receive power when the Holy Spirit has come upon you" – Acts 1:8.** The bible also says that God gives the Holy Spirit to them that ask. **(Luke 11:13)** If you are a believer and not filled, consult with your pastor or covering about taking that vital step. I talk about it more throughout the book. So, I began to minister to these two young men in the middle of Meijer. We talked for about 10-15 minutes and then I offered them prayer and they accepted. I was amazed at their willingness to accept prayer even on their job in the midst of their co-workers and other patrons. I respected their employment enough to make the prayer strong, but not lengthy.

The month was going good and I felt really joyful most of the time from witnessing to people. Witnessing is a like a breath of fresh air. Some days I would be frustrated, but then go out and minister to someone. After that, the joy of the Lord would come upon me and bring comfort to my heart. On January 5th, I went to a grocery store called Kroger. While walking up to the store, there was a young man named Romeo standing outside of the door with a petition that he was trying to get people to sign. He approached me for my signature and I approached him for Jesus. I began to minister to him and he told me that he was saved, but had just been backsliding. I prayed for him and he rededicated his life to God. He gave me his number and told me to give him a call the next day. So the next day, I called the phone number that he had given me and a young lady named Rose answered the phone. I asked for Romeo and she told me that she didn't know who I was talking about. She told me that the house was for troubled youths and that there were a lot of kids in there and she didn't know who Romeo was. So I began to minister to her. She told me that she was a Jehovah's Witness. I asked her questions about her faith, but she didn't know the answers to them. I told her about Jesus and she was susceptible to what I was saying. When I finished telling her about Jesus, she told me that she loved what I was talking about and how I was making it easy for her to understand. Rose then told me that she wanted to come to my church on Sunday. I called on Sunday and she never answered, but I 'planted the seed'.

On January 8th, Nicole and I were supposed to go out to dinner with Dorian and his wife. Nicole and I were meeting them at their house to ride with them to dinner. As we approached their house to meet with them, I saw two guys standing across the street on the sidewalk. I went inside Dorian house and they weren't ready to go yet, so I went back outside and began to minister to the two guys standing across the street. They told me that their lifestyles were totally contrary to the word of God and that they were living in sin. After conversing with them for a while, Dorian came outside and joined us. Both of them received salvation and gave their lives to Christ. All this time these two guys had been living across the street from Dorian and it wasn't until that day that the Lord set them up to be ministered to. For those who don't know what receiving salvation is, it is when you accept Jesus Christ into your life. You do this by confessing by mouth that you are a sinner, asking God for forgiveness, believing in your heart that Jesus is the son of God, believing in your heart that Jesus died and rose after three days, and allowing the Lord to take complete control of your life. On January 11th, I was working overtime and I needed a car charger. I stopped in at a liquor store but they didn't have any to fit my phone. As I walked out of the store, a woman came up to me and offered me her car charger. I walked over to her car and the Holy Spirit told me to minister to her. When you begin to live for God and receive salvation, the Holy Spirit, or God, will talk to you often, and you will hear it very clearly. I ministered to her and she received salvation. This was the first time I ministered and prayed for someone in my uniform in a public place. I was nervous, but I had to yield to the Holy Spirit.

January 14th was the first Saturday of the year that our witnessing team, the Soul Redeemers, were supposed to go out and minister throughout Fairlane Mall. We frequented Fairlane Mall a lot because the flock was always plentiful and a lot of young people patronized there. I always prayed the week before about what location the Lord wanted me to lead us to. Dorian and I were the only ones that showed up that day to minister. It didn't discourage us though, the Lord sent the disciples out in groups of twos. I understood the fact that people have busy lives, and jobs, and kids. We went throughout the mall witnessing to people. Four people had received salvation before we had finished and left the mall. After leaving the mall and walking toward our cars, we encountered an older gentleman named Brother Hayes. We were both walking by him, but at the same time the Holy Spirit moved in both of us to stop him. So, we both reached out at the same time and stopped him.

He told us that he was newly saved and that he had a problem with his heart. He told us that he was scheduled to have an emergency surgery two days from then or else he would die. Dorian and I began to pray for him and speak healing over his life. The Holy Spirit told me to tell him not to get the surgery and Dorian confirmed it. So we told him just that. We told him that he had to trust in God for a complete healing and that the Lord said that He would restore him. He didn't have a phone so we gave him a church flyer and gave him our phone numbers and told him to call us with the testimony of him being healed. We knew he would be healed. The bible says **"the prayer of faith will save the sick and the Lord will raise him up" -James 5:15.** He's mentioned further in the book.

On January 19th, I went to my dry cleaners. At that time I had been going there for almost a year. I used to always see this guy name Tyrone pressing clothes, but never talked to him. Well this one day, he was standing in the middle of the store and I approached him. He began to talk to me about how he had high blood pressure. I then began to minister to him and prayed for him in the middle of the store. The owner of the dry cleaners is a Muslim. He was about 20 feet away on the phone. God worked it out so that it wasn't until I got finished praying for Tyrone that the owner hung up the phone and walked toward us. It didn't end up being an issue and I invited Tyrone to church. Later that day, I went to my mom's house and got a chance to minister to my sister, Samantha. I ministered, and ministered, and ministered to her. She wanted to be saved, but also wanted to live in the world. She began to weep heavily and I prayed for her and comforted her and went on my way. I have ministered to her a lot. Today she is saved and fully committed to growing closer to Christ. She also attends my church. The bible teaches us that our work in the Lord is not in vain. (**1 Corinthians 15:58**). The next day on January 20th, I had worked the early shift and got off at 5:00 pm. For some reason, I was in so much pain while at work. This was my first physical attack from the 'enemy' (Satan). My whole life, I have never been sick, not even a cold. This was a new feeling for me. I didn't know how to respond. My body felt weak and I had a horrible migraine accompanied by slight dizziness. I remember getting inside the car and saying to myself that I wasn't stopping anywhere for anything. I needed gas in my car, but I had enough to make it home. As I was driving home, I was on the service drive and about to pass a gas station. I heard the Lord clearly tell me, "Stop here and get some gas". I replied, "No God, I'm not getting out of this car. I have enough gas to make it home." God then told me a second time to stop, and I reluctantly complied. I stopped at the gas station and sat there literally for about five minutes before getting out. I exited my car and went inside and paid for my gas. On my way out of the gas station, I saw this guy pumping his gas on the pump across from mine. I started pumping my gas and the Lord told me to go over and minister to the guy. I'm thinking to myself, "WHAT?" I ignored the Lord command and continued pumping my gas. When I was done pumping the gas and got ready to get back inside my car, the Holy Spirit convicted me and I went to go and minister to the guy. As I approached the man, he could tell something was wrong. He began to question me about my health and I responded, and then asked him about his salvation. He told me that he was married and had been struggling with adultery. I began to minister to him telling him how marriage is sacred and the bed is supposed to be undefiled. He began to cry and pour out tears. It seemed the more I ministered, the harder he cried. He told me that he was going to be faithful to his wife and that he needed to hear those words. After it was all said and done, he told me that he wasn't ready to give his life to Christ. But 'I planted the seed'. I went home and laid down in bed. Nicole brought me a blanket, soup, and some tea. About an hour later, I felt better. Talk about an attack from the enemy! Even though my flesh and body was weak, my Spirit was still strong. This is why it is so vital to be obedient to God and the Holy Spirit. When He says move, you have to move. If I would've ignored God and not stopped, this guy would not have gotten his breakthrough that day. It is also extremely important to be sensitive to the spirit, which comes from prayer and fasting so that you can hear God's voice when He speaks to you. Our flesh is constantly in battle with our spirit. The bible says that we either sow into the spirit or the flesh. **(Galatians 6:8)** Sowing into the spirit renders you eternal life, but the sowing into the flesh will render you death. Our goal everyday should always be to allow our spirit to grow stronger than our flesh.

4

FEBRUARY

The first month was over and it was not an easy month. Witnessing or even talking to someone everyday took some getting used to. I'm pretty sure we all encounter people on a daily basis, but not on this level. I used to see people every day at grocery stores, shopping malls, banks, work, street corners, etc., but never thought about even stopping to say 'Hi' to them. Now, I was probing into these people's personal lives. I was always lead by the Holy Spirit on who to minister to and how to minister to them. When ministering the word of God or approaching someone to witness to them, **make sure that it is of GOD.** As I said earlier, some people aren't going to be receptive to your ministering and it can turn out the wrong way. People may react with offensiveness, disrespectfulness, or even violence. If you are led by the Holy Spirit, you can't go wrong. So overall, the month of January went well and I didn't miss a day. On February 3rd, I witnessed to someone very special. He is a former Detroit police officer that was discharged after he was found guilty on some charges. When I witnessed to him, he was still a police officer and going through the judicial proceedings for his charges. He gave his life to Christ while he was going through the process. That's not to say that he gave his life to Christ just because of his predicament, it could have just been his time. When you get to that fork in the road, God already knows which way you are going to choose, but he still gives you free will to make that decision or not. This guy chose the right path when he could have went the other way. So, we talked about him being saved and living for God, and how the Lord had been dealing with him and renewing him in so many ways. Like many of you already know, a lot of the time it's not until the rain (trials) comes that you realize that you need an umbrella (God's mercy). We need to get to the point where we pull out the umbrella and prepare for the rain so that it doesn't consume us or overwhelm us. We talked for a long time and he was definitely encouraged and just wanted God's will to be done in his life. I prayed for him and then he prayed for me. This was definitely a special moment for me.

On February 8th, I ministered to a guy at the bank who told me that he had just gotten released from prison. He told me that he was a Muslim. For some reason a lot of men who get incarcerated convert to Islam and hold strong to their faith after being released from prison. This was the first Muslim that I had witnessed to on my own, so I was kind of excited and somewhat nervous at the same time. He told me that we both served the same God, just with different names. He also told me that Muhammad and Jesus were basically the same person and that Jesus was not God. I had to emphasize to him that Jesus is a deity, Muhammad is a prophet. The bible says that Jesus is God manifested in the flesh. **(1 Timothy 3:16)** He had a lot of knowledge of Islam, but I had more knowledge of Jesus. He couldn't combat my comments about Jesus or answer my questions about Muhammad. We ended up just peacefully parting our ways and agreeing to disagree. On February 10th, I witnessed to a fellow soldier while I was at drill. He told me that he was a Jehovah's Witness. We began talking and he didn't have a lot of knowledge about the Bible or about his belief. At this point, I was confused, because most Jehovah's witnesses that I had encountered study their faith strongly and this was yet another one that I witnessed to who had no idea of their own religion. After talking for a while, he told me that he just converted to a Jehovah's Witness and really didn't know too much about them. I gave him some knowledge on Jesus and just told him that he needed to study his faith more. The next day, I was at drill again, and ministered to another fellow soldier. This guy told me that he was a Catholic. I began to ask him questions about Catholicism. He couldn't give me an answer as to why he did some of the traditions that he did as a Catholic. He told me that he just does it because they tell him to. I told him just like I tell everyone else I minister to who have different beliefs, "If you're going to choose that faith or religion, make sure you know why". A lot of people choose a specific religion just because they grew up on that religion and that religion is all that they know or are used to. People also choose a religion because their significant other believes in that religion. If you are going to choose a religion, choose it because you want to. Some people choose a religion because it fits their lifestyle, while some choose a religion because they want to be accepted. When you die, you stand before God **ALONE. (2 Corinthians 5:10)** No one can intercede for you or stand in for you; not your spouse, parents, grandparents, or pastor. You have to give an account for your own life, so make sure you understand why you make that decision. After I was finished ministering to him, he seemed confused about his faith. I told him to just pray and ask God for an understanding. It is only so much knowledge and wisdom that you can give a person, the rest they have to desire and seek after themselves. The bible says that, **"of the Father and of Christ are hidden all the treasures of wisdom and knowledge". (Colossians 2:3)** I was sitting at a table ministering to him while other soldiers were around listening in. Another guy began to ask me questions about God, he was an agnostic. He told me that there wasn't a God. So I asked him how the Earth was created, and he told me that he didn't know. I just don't understand how you can deny something that makes so much sense and not have an answer to rebut it. I said, "The sun, the moon, the sky, how do you explain that being man-made?" He had no answer. I told him that he needed to do some research on religions and choose one. He told me that he would look into it. It's no sense of dying and going to Hell because of lack of knowledge. God said, **"My people are destroyed for lack of knowledge"** – Hosea 4:6.

On February 15th, I witnessed to this guy name Chris. This guy would always dance on street corners. Everyone would always laugh at him and record videos of him. So this day the Lord told me to speak to him. I asked him what was his purpose for always dancing on street corners, and he responded by saying, "this is all I know". He had no guidance. He said that his family didn't go to church and that his mom didn't care about him being out there like that. He told me dancing was his way to make money. He also told me that he wanted a job and that he wanted to go to school. I told him that God is the ultimate teacher and that He would provide for him. After ministering to him for several minutes, he told me that he wanted to come to my church. I told him that I would come and pick him up on Sunday. I even told him that if he didn't answer the phone that I would come by his house. He said, "Ok". I stayed far northwest, he stayed far southeast. It was about 30-40 minutes out of the way, but I was determined to bring willing souls with me to church every Sunday. When Sunday came, I called him multiple times and even went by his house to pick him up, but got no response. Yeah, I burned gas and wasted time, but 'I planted the seed'. The next day, I ministered to a guy who was at Meijer working. He was outside pushing shopping carts. I stopped him and asked him about his salvation. He told me that he was living with a girl that wasn't his wife. I began to minister to him. "Shacking Up" or living with someone of the opposite sex who you have an intimate/sexual relationship with is sinful. No matter how you put it, it is sin. There is no such thing as 'roommates'. Living with that person is just going to increase the lust that you already have for one another and give the enemy room to tempt you further into sin. He felt convicted and told me that he wanted to live right. I prayed for him and he gave his life to Christ and received salvation right there in the parking lot of Meijer.

On February 18th, Dorian and I went back to Fairlane mall to witness. While there, we encountered this man and woman named

Candice and Sammie who were also out there spreading the gospel of Jesus. They told me that they were out there with their church also. They told us that they had watched us pray for someone else and that they needed more boldness like we had. We began to give them advice on how to witness and how to be bolder and courageous with their witnessing. We then encountered this guy whose name I won't mention. I began to minister to him and he told us that he was saved. He also told us that he goes to church frequently. He told us that he was kind of in a hurry, but asked for my phone number so we could finish our conversation about his walk with God. He seemed like he was interested in hearing more about living righteous, so I obliged and gave him my number. Dorian and I then continued ministering throughout the mall. Fifteen minutes later, that same guy called my phone and asked what I was doing. I perplexingly told him that I was still at the mall witnessing to people. He then said, "well, ok, how long you going to be doing that?", and I responded that I didn't know. He then stated, "Well you want to meet me at the Food Café and get something to eat. I said, "No, I'm about God's business. Talk to you later. God bless you!" and hung up the phone. I told Dorian and we both just looked at each other confused. We continued witnessing throughout the mall not allowing the Devil to disturb the atmosphere. The Devil is very sneaky and conniving. He will try and make people reject you, distract you, or even get aggressive with you just to get you off track and out of the Spirit. But you must remember why you are spreading the gospel of Jesus and that it is not for you. You don't get the glory! It's for the glory of God and God alone. Don't let things distract you because it will most definitely happen. We encountered a young guy named Vincent. He was going to school at Eastern Michigan, but was staying with his girlfriend in Detroit. We gave him the gospel of Jesus on fornication and "shacking up". He received salvation and we told him that he needed to start attending church on a regular basis to stay living holy. He told us that he would come to our church that Sunday. I have heard this so many times and most of the times have had negative results, but for some reason I believed him. This was probably the most believable promise of someone coming to church that I had heard at that time. Sunday came and Dorian and I both called this guy multiple times and he was a 'no-show'. The next week, I called him and he told me that he had overslept and that he would come to church that following Sunday. That Sunday came and once again he was a 'no-show'. I called his phone and received no answer. I was really disappointed, but 'I planted the seed'. Don't let people promising you that they will come to church and not showing up discourage you. If you have a real strong heart and love for souls then sometimes it will disappoint you and upset you, but keep moving. The bible says that **"the harvest is plentiful, but he laborers are few" – Matthew 9:37**. There are many people out there in the world that need Jesus, so don't sulk and let it discourage you from inviting people to church. A couple of weeks later after witnessing at Fairlane mall, that same guy who asked me to meet him at the Food Café had called me and asked me out on a date. I quickly gave him the gospel on homosexuality and respectfully told him not to ever call my phone again. I never heard from him again. This is an issue that you might incur when giving people you minister to your phone number. Even if they are sinners and you want to help them, you never know a person's true intentions. Sinners will be sinners. I don't regret it, it was a learning experience. I would just suggest that you be led by the Holy Spirit on whom to give your phone number to, or have a separate phone number just for the people you minister to.

On February 19th, I went to work and was set to work with a fellow officer named Scott. This was my first time ever working with him. I didn't really know anything about him because we rarely talked to each other. When we got in the car, we began to drive around. About an hour into our shift, he began to tell me about problems that he was having with his wife. He seemed like he just needed to vent, so I just listened and just kept asking the Lord for a chance or

opportunity to minister to this guy. Like I said before, as police officers we are discouraged from discussing religion or politics while at
work. After about an hour of him venting, he said, "I don't know how
religious you are, but I'm trying to keep my faith". Well there you go.
Ask and you shall receive. **(Matthew 7:7)** I became elated, and he
could tell. I began to minister to him about everything dealing with
marriage and how God frowns upon divorce. We talked about God
for the remainder of the shift, which was about five hours. This was
the most I ever talked about the Lord while at work. While we were
still working I offered to pray for him after our shift was over. When
our shift ended, we both went to the locker room and he came up to
me and asked if I still was going to pray for him, and I ecstatically responded, "Absolutely yes". I prayed for him and gave him some more
words of encouragement. This was the first time I ever prayed for
another police officer while at work. He told me that he wanted to
start going to church more and reading the bible more but didn't really have a bible. I went and had a bible made for him with his name
inscribed on it and presented it to him a week later. Now he and his
wife are still happily married and doing better. On February 25th, I
was at work and had an encounter with a lady and helped her with a
situation at her house. As I was leaving, I said, "God bless you". After
hearing this, she said, "oh, you believe in God?", and I responded, "I
sure do". She then began to tell me that she had been dating this
guy who was a Muslim. She told me that she was a Christian, but he
had been talking to her about Islam. She then told me that she was
thinking about converting over to Islam for him. As I stated earlier,
you cannot risk your salvation on the account of someone else. I then
told her that he was on his way to Hell if he didn't repent and turn
to Christ and that she shouldn't follow him. She laughed and said
that she really didn't want to convert, but wasn't sure. I then told her
that I talking to her was confirmation to her own decision to remain
a Christian and just grow deeper in her faith so that she won't be
easily moved. This was just an example of how you don't need to set

up a date to go out and minister, or you don't have to plan a week in advance to minister to a person that you already know. There are always opportunities to witness to someone. Even if it's just saying, "I'm blessed and highly favored", or "God is good", or even "God bless you". These are just some things that you probably say on an everyday basis that can trigger people to begin to talk about God. This is why you must always make sure that you are ready to talk about Jesus. (**1 Peter 3:15**) You never know when your opportunity will arise. There is someone right now going through marriage problems, financial issues, unemployment, looking for love, etc. And they need your knowledge and wisdom of Jesus Christ and the Word of God to encourage and strengthen them.

5

MARCH

On March 1st, I had left my mother house and was driving down the street when I saw these four young guys walking in the street. The Holy Spirit spoke to me and told me to get out of the car and minister to them. These guys didn't look like the nicest men in the whole world, but I still heeded to the Holy Spirit. As I exited the car, one of the guys said, "what you want man?" I responded, "Just to tell y'all about Jesus". Two of them laughed, while the other two just looked at me as if I meant them harm. I began to minister to these guys and discovered that their lives were just full of sin. I began to pray for them and while doing so, the Holy Spirit told me that one of them was thinking about joining a gang. I pointed to that person and called him out, and asked him if this was true. He responded, "How did you know that?" I then told him that God loved him and had different plans for him, and that He did not want him to make that decision. He took what I said to heart and stated that he wouldn't join the gang. Could they have had guns? Yes. Could they have shot me? Yes. But like I stated earlier, you have to be obedient to the Spirit. This young guy might have joined this gang and ended up in jail or even dead if I hadn't intervened and stopped to tell them about Jesus. I personally don't take credit for any of it, it was all God. I was just a human vessel used, but he could have used anyone. I pray and hope that he really heeded to the word of the

Lord. On March 3rd, Dorian and I went to Fairlane mall again to witness. We approached a guy named Tony, who told us that he was saved and that he lives for God. He told us that he does everything in line with the word of God. So we offered to pray for him. While we were praying, the Holy Spirit revealed to me that he smokes. So I asked him, "do you smoke?" he replied, "yes, but not today. How did you know that?" (He did not have the smell of smoke on him.) I told him how I knew and told him that in order to be truly redeemed and set free that he had to get rid of that addiction. He said he would and we continued praying for him. We also ran into this man and woman who told us that they were dating and living together. We ministered to them and told them how they were living in sin. They gave us their full attention and asked many questions. They both told us that they were going to come to our church. The guy told me that he would make sure that they get up in the morning and come to church. I told the woman to give me her word that they would come because I had been lied to so many times by men on this subject. So she gave me her word that they would come to church the next day. That next day she came to church, and she was alone. She said that her boyfriend didn't want to get up, so she came on her own. I was well pleased with her veracity. That Saturday was the first time that Dorian and I went out witnessing and no one received salvation. We weren't discouraged though, 'we planted the seeds'.

On March 5th, I had an opportunity to minister to Quincy, one of my best friends. You have to wait for perfect timing to witness to family and close friends. For some reason they get easily offended and feel like you can't 'judge' them, but someone else besides you can. As a man or woman of God, we are given the authority to judge what is righteous. One of the biggest complaints I hear while ministering is that "you can't judge me". The bible says that a righteous man judges all things (1 Corinthians 2:15), and that as believers we will judge the world and even angels (1 Corinthians 6:2-3). Just make sure that you are judging that person's sins and actions and not them. You can judge the person's sin, but not the person, because we were all once sinners. So, I have learned that when it comes to family, sometimes you just have to let someone else plant the seed and you just water it. He has always gone to church and even taken me to his church a couple of times before I got saved. We talked about his lifestyle and how he was still doing the same sinful things that he and I used to do together. I didn't understand how he could see a transformation in me right before his eyes and not want to change also. He was also living with this girl that he had been dating for years in hopes of marrying her. You cannot sin in advance and think that a positive or righteous outcome will eliminate the sin. **"He that knoweth to do good, and doeth not, to him it is sin" -James 4:17.** That's like asking God for forgiveness before murdering someone or asking God for forgiveness before going over someone's house to fornicate. We talked for a while and then ended our conversation. Today he is engaged to that woman and living a more righteous lifestyle. On March 10th, I ministered to another fellow soldier while I was at drill. This is actually a real good friend of mine. I've spoken to him in the past about living righteous and letting go of his sinful lifestyle, but he continued to indulge in wickedness. So, on this day as I began to minister to him, he told me that he got ordained as a Deacon at his church. So I began to inquire about his lifestyle and asked if he was still doing the same sinful stuff as before, like porn addiction, drinking, fornication, etc. He told me that he was. How can you be a deacon and keep order in God's house if you yourself are out of order in your own house? I ministered to him and he received it, but till this day he is still living the same lifestyle.

On March 11th, I had to be at work at 11:45 pm for roll call. I was running late and for some reason I didn't witness to anyone all day. As I was pulling up to work I saw a man at the gas station across the street from my job. I looked at the clock and saw that it was 11:45 pm, but I knew if I went to roll call that I would be in there until about midnight and miss an opportunity to witness to someone. So I stopped at the gas station and ministered to this guy named Tae who struggled with smoking and drinking. He wasn't concerned about what I was saying and kept trying to change the subject, but I kept ministering. This was the closest that I had come to missing a day of witnessing. It was scary and I prayed and fasted the next day thanking God for his goodness and mercy. On March 14th, I went to Northland mall to witness to some people. I had hurt my leg playing basketball the day before, as a result I was limping as I walked throughout the mall. As I was walking this guy named Ed, who was in a wheelchair, stopped me and asked me what happened to my leg. I told him what happened to me and inquired about the reason he was in a wheelchair. He told me that something was wrong with his knee and that he had surgery and was restricted to the wheelchair. I began to minister to him and he told me that he was saved, so I prayed for him. I was on my knees in the middle of Northland mall touching and praying for this guy knee that I had never met before. Some people walked by saying, "why is he on his knees?", some just stopped and stared, while a couple of people even stretched their hands forth in agreement with the prayer. After I was done praying for him, he left and there was still some other people standing around who requested prayer. So I ministered to them and prayed for them also. It is ok to just pray for people, but you always want to know what their spiritual status is (saved/unsaved). Some people want to use your prayers to get a breakthrough or feel good about themselves, but then go right back to sinning. Sinners use God like a 'Jack-in-the-Box'. They wind Him up and ask Him for help, He pops out and helps their situation, and then they stuff Him right back in the box. So it is important before you pray for that person that you minister to them. Sometimes you won't have the opportunity to minister to them, and sometimes they won't want to hear about Jesus or salvation and only want you to pray for them. I always still pray for them, in my mind it's just a way to for the Lord to loose any strongholds that they might have and let them see the works of the Lord. Later on that day, I ministered to two guys named Lorenzo and Matthew. They told me that they were real close friends. Lorenzo told me that he was a sinner and content with it. Matthew told me that he recently gave his life to the Lord and was trying to live righteous, but struggling because the people around him. I told him that he had to cut ties with people that were not desiring to live the same holy lifestyle as him. **"Therefore, come out from them and be separate, says the Lord. Touch no unclean thing, and I will receive you" – 2 Corinthians 6:17.** This is how I see it, when you are a saved believer you already have 'demonic bullets' being thrown at you from all directions, but as believers through prayer and righteous living you are able to evade those 'demonic bullets'. What can you do if the gun (demon) is point blank range in your 'circle' and begin to shoot 'demonic bullets', how then can you evade that? I'm not saying that you shouldn't fellowship with unbelievers, but if you do, your conversation should be limited and should definitely mention Christ. Don't let unsaved people draw you back into the world with their wicked ways. I understand that sometimes you have to communicate with them on your job, or at family functions, or even at church, but keep a safe distance because the enemy knows how to lay a trap and draw you in. I invited both Matthew and Lorenzo to church, and the next Sunday Matthew came and rededicated his life to Christ. I saw him about a month later and he told me that he was abandoning all of the bad influences around him and about to go to college out of town.

On March 20th, I went to Walmart. After parking and exiting my vehicle, I began to walk toward the store entrance. I then heard some very loud profane music being played in the parking lot. I looked over a couple of aisles and saw a guy lying on the hood of a car blasting some loud music from his car radio. I stopped and just looked at him, and God said, "Go", so I went. I began praying the whole walk over to his car. When I approached him, I saw that he had a Walmart shirt on. I asked him what was going on, and he said, "Nothing, just chilling on my break". I began to minister to him about Jesus and he stopped me as soon as I started talking and turned off the radio in his car. I continued ministering to him and he said that he didn't believe in

Heaven. He then told me that he had to get back to work, so I prayed for him before he left. He was out of order blasting that profane music in a public place, but when I spoke the name of Jesus, he conformed. The Enemy trembles when he hears the name of Jesus and has to obey and act right. **(Philippians 2:10)** The Holy Spirit will always change the atmosphere. When you're on your way to work, pray and set the atmosphere so that you can have a peaceful work environment. When you're going on vacation, pray and set the atmosphere before you get there. We did it all the time before going out witnessing. We would always pray that the Lord move on the atmosphere and that the Holy Spirit would move in miracles and healings. Don't be afraid to minister to someone because of the sinful things they are doing at that time, that's the best time. There were several times that I walked up to guys holding alcoholic drinks in their hand, and when I began to minister they put the drinks down or poured them out. One time I ministered to a lady that was smoking and after I was done, she gave me her whole pack of cigarettes. You cannot be afraid of sinners or their sin when preaching the gospel of Jesus. Just always make sure that you are led by the Holy Spirit. On March 28th, after our Wednesday night Bible study, I stopped at the gas station and ministered to this guy named Lloyd. He told me that he was saved and living a holy lifestyle, but wasn't filled with the Holy Spirit. As he was speaking the Holy Spirit told me that he was hanging around someone that was doing a lot of partying. I asked him about it and he told me that his brother was a party promoter and that he attends his brother's parties regularly which are held at strip clubs and bars. I told him that situation was out of order. People think that it is okay to go to clubs and bars as long as they don't drink. There is no reason for a saved believer to be at a bar. Evil spirits cling to you, and now you have to worry about a machine gun full of 'demonic bullets' coming at you. Don't tempt yourself. God will never tempt you, or set you up for failure. The bible says that **"each person is tempted when they are drawn away by their own evil lusts/desires and enticed"** -James 1:14. I don't think that I even have to comment on the strip clubs. Here Lloyd was thinking that he was living a holy lifestyle acceptable to God, but the Lord revealed the contrary to him. That's why it is important to be filled with the Holy Ghost, especially if you are ministering to others. The Lord will reveal things to you, although some things will be kept in secret and not revealed to you. When witnessing, some people will lie to you and tell you anything just to get you out of their face, while some truly are just ignorant to their sin. Never let anyone get away with just saying, "I'm saved". Always probe deeper. Most Christians that proclaim to be saved and are living contradictory to God's word will still tell you that they are saved. A lot people don't know what 'saved' means. Most people I minister to are confused as to the meaning of salvation. Being 'saved' means that you are saved from Hell and going to Heaven. It means that you are rescued or delivered from eternal damnation. That's as clear-cut as I can put it. He told me that he couldn't stop attending the parties because he had to support his brother. I told him that one choice could lead him to Hell. We have to be careful. God withstands a lot of our abuse, but He does have limits.

On March 31st, I went to Northland mall again to witness. I ministered to this guy who called himself "KC". When I approached him, I asked him about Jesus and he became irate and started saying some weird stuff. I then asked him, "Well do you love Jesus". He replied, "Yeah I love Jesus, he is my life". The Lord then revealed to me that this guy had a tattoo of a cross on his left arm. He had on a long sleeve shirt and there were no other physical signs of tattoos present anywhere on his body. In response to his question I said, "oh and you show your love to Him by getting tattoos of Him." I then pointed to his left forearm and he lifted his shirt and revealed a tattoo of a cross and many other tattoos all over both of his arms. He marveled at the fact that I knew about his tattoo, but still let self-pride get in the way of him accepting Jesus Christ into his life. A little later, I encountered three young men. One of them rejected the gospel of Jesus and kept walking, while the other two listened carefully. While ministering, I heard the Lord clearly say to me about one of the guys, "the gates of

Heaven are closing on him". It kind of shook me a little bit because the Lord had never told me that about anyone before while I was out ministering. So, I was kind of hesitant to tell him, because just the thought of that alone was scary. I told him what the Lord told me and he gave me a frightened look. I then told him to go home and pray about it. He began to ask me questions and I told him what I thought it meant to me. I then told him **"now is the day of salvation" -2 Corinthians 6:2.** He took heed to the word of Lord and received salvation. His friend also received salvation.

6

APRIL

On April 7th, Dorian and I went to this strip mall called 7 Days West to minister to people. We talked to several people while standing at the front entrance, but many people weren't really trying to take the time to hear us. The Lord led us to leave the front entrance and walk around. So we walked around the parking lot and encountered these two guys that were sitting inside of a car. I talked to a guy name Damien, while Dorian talked to the other guy. I asked Damien if he was ready for Christ's return, and he told me that he didn't believe in the afterlife and that when he died he was going to "just be dead in the grave". I asked him if he believed in God and he told me that he did. I asked him if he believed in the bible and he replied, "yeah, but not all of it". I then told him that he couldn't pick and choose what parts of the bible to believe in, and that the bible states that there is a Heaven and a Hell. He told me that there is no proof of the afterlife. I then told him that Jesus is the living proof. I further told him that the bible says **"to be absent from the body is to be present with the Lord" -2 Corinthians 5:8.** I then asked him, "do you believe that you have a spirit?" He said, "Yeah, I got one". I said, "Well your spirit is not subject to death. When you die, your flesh dies and your body stops breathing air, but your spirit doesn't live off of air, so what happens to it?" He just looked at me and said that he didn't know. I continued ministering to him and he said that he wasn't ready to give his life to Christ. Dorian told me that the other guy wasn't receptive to the gospel either. On April 8th after our Sunday church service, I ministered to this guy named Marcus. He told me that he used to be saved but some things happened to him that caused him draw away from God. I asked, but he wouldn't go deeper into what caused him to fall away from God. He then told me that his life was just rough. While he was speaking to me the Holy Spirit quickly gave me the revelation that he had been shot in his right leg. I asked him, "you've been shot before haven't you?", and he replied, "Yeah", while raising his eyebrows and looking at me suspiciously. I then asked, "In your right leg?", and he replied, "yeah, how did you know that?" He then took a defensive stance and balled his fists. I told him that God revealed it to me. I then explained the Holy Spirit to him and the gifts of the Holy Spirit, and he told me that he never received it. The gifts of the holy spirit are: the Word of Wisdom, Word of Knowledge, Faith, Gift of Healing, Working of Miracles, Prophecy, Discerning of Spirits, speaking in Tongues, and the Interpretation of Tongues – **1 Corinthians 12:8-10.** Marcus then explained to me how being shot gave him a whole new outlook on life and on God. He blamed God for what had happened to him. I explained the story of Job to him and how Job lost everything, but still stayed faithful to God and was blessed back double the portion that he loss. I prayed for him and he rededicated his life to back to God. On April 13th, I went to a liquor store to visit two guys that I'm pretty cool with. They owned this particular store. I have known these guys for several years through my job, but never ministered to them. I started telling them how I was in the process of purchasing my new home and showed them some pictures. They started congratulating me, and there it was, 'time to minister'. I began telling them that it was all God and none of me. They began telling me how they love God and how they were Catholics. They then added that they didn't drink or smoke. I then asked them how they could serve alcohol to people if they themselves were proclaiming to be saved. They responded, "It's just a job. It's my business". How can you yourself be saved, but watch all these people around you struggling with addictions and possibly on their way to Hell. And not just that, but help them go to Hell by selling them all that wickedness (lottery tickets, condoms, liquor, porn). I just couldn't get it. So after probing deeper trying to get an understanding, they revealed that they weren't filled with the Holy Spirit. That explained it all. The Holy Spirit brings forth conviction. It causes you to feel uncomfortable when there is sin occurring around you and in your presence. It also causes you to speak up against that same sin. I just prayed that God would make a way financially and give them provision to get out of the business that they were in.

On April 21st, Dorian and I went to Fairlane mall again to witness. When Dorian and I first got there, Dorian had to go to the bathroom, so we went. While we were walking up to the restroom, we ran into Brother Hayes, the guy that we ministered to and prayed for with the heart issue on January 14th. We began to talk to him and he told us that he took our advice and didn't go and get the surgery. He told us that when he went back to the doctor they told him that they didn't see the problem anymore and that he was healed. GLORRRYYYYY!!!!!! How many people know that God is a healer! He trusted in God for his healing and God rewarded him for his faithfulness. After leaving the restroom, we saw these two young guys that we wanted to minister to across the mall. As we approached them, the Holy Spirit told me the first letters of their names. I pointed to one guy and said, "Your name is C", and then I pointed at the other guy and said, "And your name is J". They both looked at each other and said, "What? Stop playing, how did you know that?" Their names were Corey and Javon. I began to tell them about the Holy Spirit and minister salvation to them. The whole time we were ministering, they were still standing there with a surprised look on their faces. After ministering to them they still asked me how I knew their names. Javon received salvation, while Corey told me that he wasn't ready. I am telling you, miracles and wonders will move people to draw closer to God. We left them and began ministering to these three young boys. They were all like

14 years old. They told us how they didn't know about God and how they weren't raised in church and used that as an excuse for their sin. I told them that God wants everyone to be saved and to come into the knowledge of truth - **(1 Timothy 2:4).** They began telling us how they were fornicating with girls and starting to drink. Then Dorian began telling them how they were living an unholy lifestyle that would lead them to Hell, not Heaven. At first they were laughing and being goofy, but after hearing that word 'Hell', they straightened up and became attentive. People don't want to hear about Hell, only Heaven. They don't want to hear about where their wickedness will lead them. You cannot be afraid to tell people the truth about where there sins will lead them. You have a spiritual obligation to shed your light onto others. The bible says, **"let your light so shine before men, that they may see your good works and glorify your God in Heaven" – Matthew 5:16.** We finished talking and praying for them and moved on. We then encountered this guy who told us that he was a Catholic, but stated that he really didn't follow any of their practices. We ministered to him and he gave his life to Christ and received salvation. That was the Holy Spirit moving on that young man. What we explained to him in twenty minutes about Jesus made more sense to him then his twenty five years of being a Catholic.

On April 24th, I went back to the liquor store that I mentioned earlier to buy some non-alcoholic champagne to celebrate Nicole birthday. As I was leaving, I saw a guy named Pat outside drinking a beer at his car, which was parked right next to mine. I approached him and began to minister to him and he said, "How you going to tell me about my drink and you got a drink in your hand", I laughed. I had the bottle inside a paper bag that was also inside of a plastic bag, but he saw the top of it. I showed and explained to him what it was and continued ministering to him. He received salvation right there in front of the liquor store. He told me that he wanted Jesus right there and then, regardless of the fact that his friends were sitting across the street in the open field watching me pray for him. This was a good experience, but it really made me pay even closer attention to the things that I do when I am out in the world. For some reason the 'world' looks for opportunities to criticize Christians. Sinners spend more time talking about why they don't go to church then why they should. They also spend more time trying to negate the Word of God than trying to understand it. Most of all, they spend so much time finding reasons not to serve God and live a holy lifestyle then they spend trying to find reasons to serve God and live righteous. And I know this because I used to be just like this! Sinners are quick to judge a saint, but even quicker to get offended when a saint judges them. So we have to watch what we do, because sinners are definitely watching what we are doing! Be careful of what movie you are going to watch at the theaters, or what kind of music you are listening to in front of people, or what kind of clothes you are wearing. Ultimately everything you do is between you and God, and if he tells you it's cool to see certain movies, or listen to certain music, or wear certain clothes, then so be it. Just be careful not to do certain things around sinners, because they don't understand the voice of God and will perceive it wrongfully. Understand that when people look at you, they should be able to see the God in you. You might be the only Jesus that these sinners see, so make Jesus look good! Sinners look for reasons to doubt our faith just to add to the reasons they live unholy. Some of the attacks against the church that I hear a lot are, "churches only care about your money", or "pastors cheating on their wives", or "all church people do is gossip". These are all excuses not to join a church or live righteous. You are not giving your tithe money to a pastor, but you are giving it unto God and by the way, **GAS AND LIGHTS ARE NOT FREE.** There are many churches out here that are living righteous and have Holy Spirit filled pastors that are faithful to their families. There are also churches that have members that show love, instead of gossiping, and my church is one of them. You have to seek out after a church and find the one that's suitable for you. Not suitable meaning that you sit in the back and hope that the pastor doesn't call you out, but suitable so that it refines you and molds you to be a righteous man or woman of God. This can only be done by prayer and fasting. If you are already in a church, sit still until the Lord tells you to move. Don't go running away real fast because you see things going wrong, you might be the one to change that wrongdoing. I know many people that 'church hop' and never allow the anointing of God to move upon them. Sit still and allow the Lord to move on you and use you for His house. **"Those who are planted in the house of the Lord, shall flourish in the courts of our God" –Jeremiah 92:13.**

On April 30th, I went to the Secretary of State to take care of some business for my vehicle. While I was waiting in line, I began to talk to the security guard there. Shortly after, I began to minister to him. He started telling me that a lot has happened in his life, but he was still trying to trust in God through it all. He told me that he really didn't want to go into detail about it, but that was the reason why he wasn't living righteously before the Lord. He told me that he wanted to live righteous, but it was just hard to. So I continued ministering to him, and eventually led him outside of the building where I prayed for him. He gave me his number and I called him a couple days later. When I called and talked to him, he began to weep and tell me how scared he was of the Devil. He told me that his wife had died a couple years ago and he had been having a lot of strange and weird things happen to him that he believed were demonic. He told me that he was on the brink of a nervous breakdown and confused about what he needed to do. I began to minister to him and pray for him. I told him that the first step was for him to get saved and give his life over to the Lord, because once he gets saved he would possess power over the Devil and his atmosphere. He began to weep even harder and harder. So I began to pray harder and harder. I invited him to church and he visited a couple of weeks later and received salvation. It is important that you know that ministering is not just about planting a seed and forgetting about it. Don't you want to see your seed grow and blossom into a beautiful and fruitful tree? Well you have to do more. You just don't want to plant a seed and walk away and leave it unattended, because then a wild bird (the Devil) will come and eat that seed. Stay in constant contact with the people you minister to, especially if they aren't saved. If feasible, get their phone number, address, email, or even Facebook account, whatever you can to try and stay in contact with them. The first time you meet a person, they most likely aren't going to tell you about their whole life or their deepest secrets, but on the phone or on your next conversation they might be more susceptible to reveal things to you. The Lord has blessed me with a gift of ministering to people to where they feel comfortable opening up to me, but it's not always like that. You have to stay in contact with these people because they are just walking around dead and the devil is seeking to destroy them, but your goal should be to help them receive life. **(John 10:10)** If they reject you repeatedly, then it's nothing you can do. When I witness to people, they give me many excuses, like they don't have a phone, or they just moved to a new address. There's nothing you can do except give them a church flyer, invite them to church, and make sure you add them to your prayers. If I would have just left this guy that day without getting his phone number, who knows where he would be to-day. By me getting his number and being able to probe further, I was able to get him the help that he needed from Christ and help see him through a tough time is his life. Keep in mind, you never know what someone is going through in their life. We live in a tough economy. There are many people that are one argument away from going on a killing spree, or one bill away from committing suicide. Get to know these people, they need Jesus, we all need Jesus!

7

MAY

On May 3rd, while I was working, I saw these three teenagers walking up the street. I stopped and began ministering to them. They were confused about life and religion. They had no idea what to believe in, but they were very interested in what I had to say. They wanted to know how I was able to live a holy lifestyle being so young. I told them that it wasn't about age, but maturity. When you first get saved, you are a "reborn" in Christ, 'a little child'. The bible says that once you become saved you are a new creation -2 **Corinthians 5:17.** God wants us to come to him as little children, humble and attentive, wanting and willing to learn. I told them that when I first got saved, it wasn't easy. I faced many trials and tribulations, but I persevered through them because I loved God. You have to desire to have a personal relationship with Jesus. I told them that it wasn't until I got fully saved and filled with the Holy Spirit that it became easy. When you are a little child in Christ, you think like one, but once you become mature in the things of God, you put away those child-like thoughts. **(1 Corinthians 13:11)** They wanted to know more and more, but at this time their parents had walked down the street and started inquiring if they were in trouble since they saw the police car and me out there talking to them. I prayed for them and let them go, but not without getting their phone numbers and inviting them to church. They gave me their word that they would come to church service that following Sunday. I doubted them seeing that I have heard this so many times. When I called them the night before Sunday, their mom answered the phone and thought that I was a drug dealer because of my deep voice. I told her who I was and why I was calling and she was elated. She apologized to me and told me that her sons had been getting into a lot of trouble and hanging out with the wrong crowd. I talked to them and they gave me their word that they would be waiting for me to pick them up the next day. I was only able to get in contact with the two of them that lived together. They stayed pretty far from me, about thirty minutes out of the way. When Sunday came, I called them multiple times and didn't receive an answer, but I still went in faith to go and pick them up. When I pulled up in front of their apartment building, they were outside waiting. Glory to God! Talk about faith! I took them to church and one of them received salvation and gave his life to the Lord.

On May 5th, I went to Fairlane mall again. The first guy that I and Dorian ministered to was angry and didn't want to listen to us. He ignored all of our questions and just wanted to leave. We weren't holding him in handcuffs, he could of left, but for some reason he stayed there and kept talking to us. The Holy Spirit told me that he had girl and that they had been arguing. When I brought this to his attention, he stopped, looked at us and got angrier. He then began to talk about how she made him mad. He told us about the argument that they had gotten into. We began to minster to him about the situation while still ministering salvation to him. We encouraged him and strengthened him and told him that if that girl was for him, no other man could have her. What God has for you, is for you! He started crying and saying that he loved her. I told him that he had to first serve God and develop a relationship with Him if he expected any type of happiness or joy in any other type of relationship. We ministered to him a little more and prayed for him and let him go.

On May 7th, a couple of co-workers and I went to Ponderosa Steakhouse to get something to eat. When I entered, I saw a young lady working at the cash register. I am kind of hesitant when it comes to ministering to women, due to the fact that they often perceive it wrongly and think that I am making advances toward them. Dorian and I used to run into that problem often when attempting to minister to women. It's different when you are a woman trying to minister to a man. But if you are a man trying to minister to a woman, I have found it easy just to make sure that the first thing that comes out of your mouth is God or Jesus. It works, or it at least gets there attention in a different kind of way. I felt the Holy Spirit tugging on me to minister to her badly, so I did. She told me that she had really been struggling with fornication, clubbing, and trying to find a man. I began ministering to her and telling her the attributes of a Godly woman. I also began telling her how her body is a holy temple and is supposed to be undefiled and set aside for her husband. One of the biggest complaints that I have received from single women while ministering to them is that they are tired of waiting for God to send them a man, or that they keep running into the wrong types of guys. I want every single woman reading this book right now to know that once you come into Christ, you are holy and sanctified and your temple belongs to him. The bible says that you are a beautiful and precious jewel **(Proverbs 31:10)**. As a single woman, you should wait on God to send the perfect man your way. I know that it can be hard waiting, and can also be lonely, but the bible tells us to **"don't grow weary in well doing, you shall reap in due season if you faint not"- (Galatians 6:9)**. As a single woman, it is not your job to seek after a man, but it is a man's job to find you. The bible says, **"He who finds a wife finds a good thing, and obtains favor from the Lord" –Proverbs 18:22**. I say again, it is a man job to find you, do not seek after a man. You are probably single because the Lord isn't through working on YOU, or He isn't through working on your MAN. The Lord probably still has to change you spiritually, emotionally, or even physically. A woman's heart should be so hidden in God that a man has to seek Him just to find her. So please open up your eyes women and stop losing your-self and pulling yourself farther away from the Lord to chase after a man. She listened to all the things that I had to say and I gave her a tract. For those of you who don't know, a tract is a small pamphlet that contains bible literature. There are many different tracts that contain different literature on different subjects. I use these a lot while witnessing to people. They come in handy and are effective, especially when you have that person who just walks away from you and don't want to hear anything about Jesus. They also really come in handy when you try and minister to that person that is in a hurry and don't have time to talk to you. I encounter a lot of those people who give me that excuse. There were a lot of times I was in a hurry to get somewhere, but duty called for me to minister about Jesus to someone. It's all about your dedication and sacrifice. The bible tells us to present our bodies as a living sacrifice, holy and acceptable to God, which is your reasonable service. **(Romans 12:2)** It says, "which is your reasonable service". It is your 'reasonable service' or duty to minister to people. That's the least we can do for our savior that died on the cross for us, for our savior that was beaten and humiliated all day and night so that we may be free. The bible tells us to use our gifts that we have been given to minister to others. **-1 Peter 4:10**

On May 11th, I had the opportunity to minister to this guy that I have known since I was a little kid. He is a recovered drug addict. When I was young he used to be real heavy into drugs and sex. He recently gave up the addiction and was trying to live for God. He said that he was saved and living righteous. I began to probe further into his walk with God, like I do everyone I minister to, and found out that he was still struggling in some major areas. He told me that he was still struggling with fornicating with many random women. If you are struggling with some lifestyle changes like the movies you watch, the way you dress, or the music you listen to, that's one thing. When you get saved and give your life to Jesus, some things in your life will take time to change for some people. It is definitely not an overnight experience. But when you struggle with things like fornicating, drunkenness, stealing, and other **sinful** things, now you are struggling with sin. I'm not saying that just because you get saved that major battles or sin like this will immediately stop or you will become perfect. That's not the case. The Lord still has to create a renewing spirit within you, but you cannot become content with that sin. He told me that he stopped doing drugs and felt like that was enough. His excuse was that he came from a long way and that he can't change everything. He told me that he had been drug free for almost two years. So I asked him, "How long do you think it will take for you to change the other sinful things in your life?" He told me, "When it happens, it will happen". God doesn't want part of you, He wants all of you. He wants you completely sold out for Him. You cannot give God your whole body, but keep your toes in the world. That's like getting married and keeping old phone numbers of the people you used to date. **Because you are lukewarm, and neither cold nor hot, will I vomit you out of my mouth –Revelation 3:16.** An excuse that I hear a lot from people who proclaim to be saved is that they are saved, but they're just 'backsliding'. The term backsliding is a term often used by Christians to describe a process by which an individual who has given their life to God reverts back to old habits and/or lapses or falls into sin. It can also mean when a person turns from God to pursue their own sinful desire. Some people use this word as an excuse to continue in their sinful ways. They feel like they can become content in their sinful ways and continue to sin and God will still always love them and accept them into Heaven. This isn't completely true. While it is true that God always loves us and wants us all to come into repentance **(2 Peter 3:9)**, He still knows that we can overcome sin. The bible says that the same temptations and sin that we struggle with daily, Jesus was also faced with and sinned not. **(Hebrews 4:15)** If we ought to be Christ-like, how then can God be willing to accept us falling away from Him and becoming content in our wicked ways? Once you have tasted the sweetness of God and are eating well spiritually and wearing new Heavenly garments, how can you go back to the same vomit that you left? I'm not saying that you can't make a mistake and sin, but you have to be quick to repent. I told him that once he tempts himself and indulges in the same sin that he left, that unclean spirit will come back to attack him with seven more stronger demons. (**Matthew 12:45**) After ministering to him, he told me that he liked the conversation and definitely wanted to continue it. I talked to him again and he told me that he was doing better in his walk with God and that he had cut a lot more sinful things out of his life.

On May 21st, I encountered this guy named Rashad. He told me that he had just started going to church two weeks before that day. I asked him what made him start going to church and he told me that he wanted to live right. He told me that no one ministered to him or told him about God, but that he started going to church out of his own volition. This was the first time I have ever encountered anyone who started attending church on their own. Most people have someone minister to them or are invited to a church. He told me that the church he was at didn't offer him salvation. He also told me that he really didn't know about the church and their practices. I began to minister to him and told him what living holy was really about. He told me that he had been struggling with some worldly things and that the church wasn't helping him through it. I prayed for him and he received salvation.

On May 25th, the Enemy attacked my body again and I was really sick. I was vomiting all day and felt really cold while it was a very hot day. Nicole helped me into bed and bought me soup again. Through my sickness, I hadn't witnessed to anyone that whole day. A little later, much to Nicole's despise, I got up out of bed and drove to Meijer to witness to someone. I found myself driving to Meijer a lot to minister to people. Whenever a day had gone by without me ministering to anyone, I found myself there. When I got there I saw a guy that worked there out in the parking lot pushing baskets. I talked to him and began to minister to him. I almost vomited while I was talking to him. I was freezing cold out there ministering to him with a jacket on, while he was wearing a short sleeve shirt. He asked me why I was outside in the condition that I was in, and I told him, "Because people need Jesus". I didn't care about my sickly condition, I had to do God's will. The Apostle Paul went throw many afflictions and many shipwrecks but stayed on the course to minister the gospel of Jesus. I continued ministering to him, but then he began to breakdown and tell me about how he was a sinner. I comforted and prayed for him and he received salvation. Mission accomplished. My spirit was uplifted and I began to physically feel better also.

On May 27th, I went to Home Depot with my mother. While we were walking around shopping, this guy offered us help. After he helped us, I offered him help with Jesus. We began to talk and he told me that he loved God and had been desiring to live for Him, but sin seemed so much more soothing and easier. I began to minister to him while he was still working. Most people that you are going to minister to aren't going to be fresh and new to sin. Most of them are going to have a sinful mindset that has been controlling them for a while. You have to break past that wickedness and minister holiness to them. That's why people are so quick to say, "You are judging me", because all they know and are comfortable with is sin. So when you come to them with some new knowledge, they get offended and think that you are trying to compare yourself with them. But **"the word of God is living and powerful, and sharper than any two-edged sword, piercing even to the division of soul and spirit, and of joints and marrow, and is a discerner of the thoughts and intents of the heart" –Hebrews 4:12.** As you begin to minister the Word of God to them, the old past sinful knowledge that they have will begin to breakdown in their spirit. The problem is that when most people leave your presence, they don't hold fast to the word of God, but instead open up their heart and spirit to that same wickedness that was just starting to breakdown within them. After ministering to him, he told me that he wanted to give his life to Jesus and live righteous. He told me that he had some bad influences in his life that had to go. I prayed for him and he received salvation. The next day, I was driving down the street and saw a man and a younger teen walking in the middle of the street. I stopped the car and got out to minister to them. The two were father and son. I began to talk to them and the father told me that his son had been facing some challenges in school. He also told me that he was hanging around the wrong crowds and smoking. So then I asked the father, "and what are you doing?" He told me that he also smokes. I then told him, "So don't be the first to throw stones". Here this man was trying to crucify his son and throw his son 'under the bus', when he was just as bad if not worse. I began to minister to them both. The son was more knowledgeable in the things of God than the father was. The son told me that he was facing a lot of pressure at school and that he loved to smoke illegal drugs. The father told me that he wanted the best for his son, but that he himself never tried to get him into a church or urge him to live a holy lifestyle. I told the father that he had to be right for his son. The bible tell us to train up our children in the right things of God, and when they get older they will not depart from it. **(Proverbs 22:6)** I then began to pray for them both. While I was praying, the Holy Spirit revealed to me that they weren't close at all. So I began to pray that they have a closer relationship and also prayed for better communication between the father and mother. When I was finished praying, I looked up and the father eyes were pouring out with tears. I asked him what was wrong, and he told me that he and his son haven't been spending a lot of time together because he wasn't a good father. He also told me that the boy's mother had been keeping their son away from him, but he was desiring for a closer relationship between him and his son. They were amazed at the fact that I knew their current situation and began to say that God must be real. They then told me that they wanted to live for God and they both received salvation.

8

JUNE

During this time, Nicole and I were down to only one vehicle. On June 9th, Dorian and I were supposed to go to Fairlane mall to witness. Dorian was already there and I was running late due to heavy traffic. While I was driving, a vehicle two cars in front of me slammed on his brakes causing a four-car accident. The accident had ruined the whole front end of my car and it was not drivable. I wanted to scream and yell knowing that this was the only means of transportation for me and my wife, but instead I put myself in a place of peace and began to call on Jesus. God said, **"For I know the thoughts that I think toward you, thoughts of peace and not of evil, to give you a future and a hope" –Jeremiah 29:11.** I called Dorian and told him what happened, and him being faithful came to pick me up and sat with me until the tow truck came and impounded my vehicle. Dorian then drove me over my mother house so I could use her extra vehicle. While we were driving, we saw these two guys walking up the street. Dorian and I exited his car and began to minister to them. They told us that they were sinners and proud of it and that they had no idea of what living holy was. We gave them the knowledge on Jesus and prayed for them. As we were getting back inside the vehicle, two guys that they knew walked up to them and I heard them telling the other guys about Jesus. Believe it or not, whenever you minister to someone, it is an encounter that they will never forget, especially if you just walk up to them randomly on the street or at a mall. People don't usually just walk up to other people and start talking so they will remember your audaciousness. I could have moped around and just have been sad about my vehicle, but instead Dorian and I still found it within us to minister. On June 20th, Nicole and I left Wednesday night bible study and stopped at the gas station to get some gas. I am really thankful for Nicole. I really thank her for her patience and diligence in dealing with my witnessing. She was very understanding and supportive of me stopping a lot when we were together to minister to people. I witnessed at gas stations a lot, I mean after all, we all need gas right? That just shows how many opportunities we all have to minister. Think about it! I'm pretty sure everyone reading this book has a car or has had a car at some point in their lives. You have to stop and get gas at some point, so why not minister while pumping gas. It's the perfect place! A person can't leave until there gas is finished pumping, so that kills the "I'm in a rush" excuse. Plus, people just stare at each other anyway while pumping their gas. This was always the perfect spot for me to find souls to minister to, people were always at the gas station at all times of the day. While there, I saw this guy pumping his gas and I approached him to minister to him. When I approached him, he pulled the nozzle out of the gas tank and pointed it at me. I laughed and then told him that I just wanted to talk to him about Jesus. He said, "Oh ok". I began to minister to him and he told me that he was struggling with sexual lusts. This was the problem with most men that I encountered. I told him that if he loved his girlfriend that he would wait on her and not fornicate with her. I prayed for him and then left the gas station.

On June 24th, after Sunday service I went outside the church and ministered to this lady named Ciara. She told me that she wasn't saved and struggling with homosexuality. I ministered to her and invited her to church. She promised that she would come to church that following Sunday, but she didn't come. I saw her several weeks later and asked what happened to her coming to church and she told me that she got busy, so I invited her again. She still didn't come, but I had seen her several weeks after that. When I saw her, I asked her again what happened to her coming to church and she gave me another excuse. I invited her again and still had negative results. One day I was driving up the street and I began ministering to a guy, and while I was ministering to him, the same lady, Ciara, walked up. She told me that the guy I was ministering to was her brother, and that they were going to come to church that following Sunday. Every time I invited her to church, I offered her a ride, even though the church was two blocks away. Every time she declined my offer for a ride, as well as that time. She never showed up that following Sunday. I think that it is just crazy how you can minister to the same people and they constantly lie to you. But that's what people do to God. They continuously tell God, "I'm going to do better", or "I'm going to live for you", or "I'm going to stop sinning". They say, "God, I love you", but spit in His face. When you sin, that's exactly what you are doing. You say, "God forgive me for my sins", then God forgives you and you turn around and do the same thing. How long do you expect God to continuously sit and let you spit in His face? It comes a point where God gets sick of the disrespect and takes a stand. Don't get me wrong, the Lord will continuously have unconditional and everlasting love for you, but not for your sin. **"For the eyes of the LORD are on the righteous, and His ears are open to their prayers; But the face of the LORD is against those who do evil" -1 Peter 3:12.** Don't get to the point where God begins to ignore your prayers. Let Him know that he can trust you.

On June 30th, Dorian and I went back to Fairlane Mall to witness. The first person that we encountered was a guy named Deron. Dorian asked him if he knew about Jesus and he responded with, "yeah, I know about him and so what". He told us that he believed in God, but didn't believe in the bible. He asked Dorian, "What is truth?" and followed by saying that truth is what you make it. He then said that everything in the bible isn't true. And then further asked us who wrote the bible and how we knew that it all was true. Dorian asked him an excellent question, "who was the first president?" he responded, "George Washington". Then Dorian asked, "how do you know if that is true?", and he responded, "because it is written in books." Dorian replied, "Well there you have it". Deron then became upset because Dorian refuted his statement and became irate. He and Dorian started getting loud and going back and forth about which one of them was right. I then stopped Dorian and told him to leave it alone. The bible tells us to avoid foolish and ignorant disputes, knowing that they generate strife. **(2 Timothy 2:23)** The bible also tells us to shun profane and idle babblings because they will only lead to more ungodliness **-2 Timothy 2:16.** There was no point of us standing there arguing with someone which was only going to cause a commotion. Most people that are like that only want one thing, and that is to prove that they are right. They don't care about reasoning or evidence. Most people like that just have an argumentative spirit and just love to argue because it excites them. Dorian and I always did a good job with not pushing people to their limits or upsetting people, but this one guy for some reason was very upset and aggressive. This is why it is important to go out witnessing as a group, or at least as in groups of twos. There are many reasons for you to go out with another person. When you go out with another person you can be accountable for one another; one person may have teaching gifts while the other has practical gifts, or both; there is also greater power – **"Again I say to you that if two of you agree on earth concerning anything that they ask, it will be done for them by My Father in Heaven. For where two or three are gathered together in my name, I am there in the midst of them" –Matthew 18:19-20.** And last but not least, with another person out there with you, you'll always have someone to watch your back. Dorian and I were a great duo. He had a lot of biblical knowledge and knowledge of other religions and I had a lot of tact. Even after all the confusion and aggressiveness from this guy, we still offered him prayer, and he accepted.

Like I stated earlier, people want prayer just not the added 'stuff' that comes with it. We prayed for him and continued witnessing through-out the mall. The next two guys we ministered to had no knowledge of the bible at all, but still wanted to debate with us. These two young men were telling us what they <u>thought</u> the bible said. I have run across a lot of sinners who create scriptures to support their sin. The bible tells us to be holy in all of our conduct. **(1 Peter 1:15)** There is nothing holy about sin and there are no scriptures that are going to support sinfulness. We prayed for these two guys and moved on. After these couple of encounters, it seemed like the mall had a rough crowd, but we continued. We wanted to encounter those people that were ignorant to the Word and those that were the closest to Hell. We encountered two more young guys. One of the guys rejected us right when we approached them and mentioned Jesus, while the other stayed and listened. He told us that he was in a hurry, but that he did want to live holy but just didn't know how. We ministered to him and walked him through the path of righteousness. I guess the spirit of God moved on him because he was no longer in a hurry, but instead began to listen and ask questions. After all was said and done, he received salvation.

9

JULY

On July 2nd, I went to Northland Mall to minister to people. While there, I talked to four young guys, and after speaking with them found out that they were all living sinful lifestyles without Jesus and on their way to Hell. Can you imagine the impact you can make if you helped one person to receive salvation? They can then go back to their group of friends and get them saved, and each of those friends can get their circle of friends saved, and so on, and so forth. Look at Paul, who before his conversion was known as Saul, who persecuted saints. He received salvation and became one of Jesus' greatest disciples, helping millions of other people get saved. Here were these for guys and none of them knew about Jesus. One of the guys told me that he was a Christian, but was studying to become a Muslim. I didn't understand how he could study a different religion without first studying his own religion. I asked him, "How do you know that Christianity isn't the right religion for you if you know nothing about it", he replied, "I think I know enough". I gave him knowledge on Islam and Christianity and told him to study up on both of them and make his decision. I prayed for them and let them go. On July 4th, I was working downtown at the Salvation Army. I ministered to these three older men that were recovering drug attics. Two of them told me that they were still struggling with sex and felt that it was alright because they were set free from drugs. I told them that they could not be partially set free and that it wasn't possible. If you stop sinning in some ways but continue to sin in other ways, you are still a sinner, and unless you repent, you will not inherit the kingdom of God. I am not referring to a quick overnight transformation, but rather not becoming content in a continuous sinful nature. They listened and told me they both told me that it was hard because they lived on the street and that it was temptation all around them. I then told them that was just an excuse to sin. You don't have to become a product of your environment. You can definitely take a stand against sin. People use the saying, "love makes you do crazy things". Well I agree, the love that you have for God should be crazy and should be demonstrated through your hatred for sin. These guys told me that they were appreciative of the knowledge that I gave them.

On July 10th, I was shopping at Burlington when I encountered two young men named Jordan and Devin. The Lord told me to minister to them, but I was very hesitant for some reason. Usually when I'm at the mall or grocery store shopping, I look for people to minister to just because it's so many sinners in these places. I listened to the Lord and walked over to them and began to talk to them. At first Jordan was kind of standoffish, while Devin was attentive as to what I was saying. I began to minister to them after they told me that they weren't saved. Jordan told me that he had a scholarship to play college football. However, he didn't think that he could handle being saved because there would be a lot of temptation coming his way. He didn't know it, but he was speaking sin into his life. **"For as he thinks in his heart, so is he" – Proverbs 23:7.** He then asked me if it was possible for him to live holy while in college, and if so how he could do it. I told him the scripture **Psalms 119:9 – "How can a young man cleanse his way? By taking heed according to Your word."** There is power in the word of God, and it is filled with a lot of knowledge for people to take in. He told me that was something that he was going to think about. I continued ministering to them and then prayed for them. While I was praying for them, the Lord told me that demons were after Jordan, and that they wanted him bad. I heard this from God very forceful and very clear. I stopped praying, looked up at Jordan and my eyes watered up and began to fill with tears. He looked at me with a concerned look on his face. I felt so scared for this young man that it had led me to tears. In all of my experience out ministering to people, I had never heard this from God. As a disciple of Christ, sometimes the Lord will give you a good word and sometimes a bad one, you have to be prepared to deliver whatever type of word that you receive from God. I most definitely wasn't prepared for this. I didn't even know how to tell him this, nevertheless how he would receive it. I told him what the Lord said to me and he frowned up and asked me, "why me?" I told him that I didn't know why, but that he should definitely take heed to it. He then began to ask me what he should do. He told me that he wanted to have fun in college. I told him that God will show him the path of life; and that in His presence is fullness of joy; and at His right hand are pleasures forevermore. **(Psalms 16:11).** He then said, "All that church stuff is cool, but what do I do?" I then told him, "live for God and die to sin, or else the Devil will devour you". It even sounded scary to me coming out of my mouth, so I knew that it sounded scary to him. I then prayed for him again and rebuked all demonic attacks that were coming his way. He still didn't want to receive Christ into his life, but 'I planted the seed'.

On July 14th, I ministered to this much older guy named Holmur. I saw him walking to his car from Rite Aide. When he walked by me, it appeared that he had been drinking because of his stagger-ing walk. I followed him to his car and began to talk to him. He told me that he wasn't a drinker and that he was walking like that because of some medicine that he was on. I looked in the car and saw a pint of liquor. He then confessed to me that he had been drinking. I have always been hesitant about ministering to older people due to the fact that most of them feel like they know more than you. Older people are usually very stubborn when it comes to listening to someone younger than them. I began to minister to him, and he told me that he also smokes and fornicates. He then told me that he was still going to Heaven though. I didn't know how to tell him that he was not on the right path to Heaven. So I gave him the scriptures, **Psalms 7:11- God is a just judge, and God is angry with the wicked every day** and **Psalms 9:17- The wicked shall be turned into Hell, and all the nations that forget God.** He said, "Oh well in that case I guess I'm not going to Heaven". He was honest, but I told him that he still had a chance. I told him how to repent and receive salvation. He then told me that he wasn't ready, but that he would visit my church. I definitely would had never thought this guy would of came due to the fact that he was drunk while I was talking to him and not really paying attention, but much to my surprise, he visited the church that following Sunday. So remember just because someone looks like they aren't serious about God doesn't mean that they really aren't. Just because they don't have a car and are homeless, still doesn't mean that you shouldn't invite them, you never know. It became a habit for me, that everyone I ministered to, I invited them to church. On July 22nd, I was working in the cell block on my job doing suicide watch. That is when you sit in a chair and watch a particular person who is locked up all night because they are a suicide risk. I was watching this lady who was arrested for shooting someone. While I was sitting back there, this lady started talking to me. This was ironic because she had been locked up for three days at that time and told me that many other officers had come back there to watch her but she never said *a word* to them. She told me about her struggles; how she had multiple kids and was trying hard to provide for them, how she couldn't find a job, etc. So I asked her if she was saved and she told me that she used to be saved, but that she currently was not. So I began to minister to her and told her that she needed to trust God through *every* trial and tribulation, not just some. **"Behold, I am the LORD, the God of all flesh. Is there anything too hard for Me?" (Jeremiah 32:27)** She told me that it was hard because she might be facing time in jail. I then told her, "If God will see you to it, He will see you through it" and told her **Psalms 3:3 -But**

You, O LORD, are a shield for me, My glory and the One who lifts up my head. I ministered to this lady for the next six hours of my shift until it was time for me to get off. When I was getting ready to leave, I offered her prayer. This was a problem. Like I stated earlier, my job didn't want us talking about religion to each other, nevertheless a prisoner. But I was definitely led by the Holy Spirit, so I was obedient to God and prayed for her and uplifted her. She will never forget that day and neither will I.

On July 28th, Dorian and I went to this strip mall called Value Save Plaza to witness. While there, we encountered these two guys named Justin and Cory. Cory was a younger guy. We began to minister to these guys and Justin told us that he fornicates and smokes marijuana all the time, but that God loved him and was still going to let him into Heaven. I asked him if he used needles to do heroin, and he told me that he didn't. I then asked, "so if someone came to your house and said let me in so I can do this heroin in your house, what would you say?" he replied, "no, go down the street and do that, you not doing it in my house". I then told him that God is the exact same way. You can't come and knock at His door and say, "let me in so I can fornicate and smoke in your house". God is going to reply, "No, not here in My house". He laughed and said, "That was a good one man. I guess I see where you coming from." God's house is not a regular house, it is a holy Kingdom. That means that you can't break in, or sneak in like you would a regular house, there is only one way in and that is through Jesus. There are no side windows or back door entrances into Heaven. While I was talking to Justin, Dorian was talking to Cory. I overheard their conversation somewhat and Cory stated that he just didn't know what route in life to take. He said that all his friends were sinners and living crazy lives, but he knew that he didn't want to be like them. Dorian began to tell him about living holy and overcoming evil with good. Dorian and I both prayed for them and they both received salvation. Dorian and I also ministered to this young man and woman that were dating.

The Lord led Dorian to stop them and pray for them and their child that they had, but I had other intentions. We began to talk to them about salvation. We learned that they had been dating for years and living together. We asked them if they were getting married and they said, "Yeah soon". We talked to them about marriage and fornication and then prayed for them. While we were praying the Lord gave me revelation that they had been having huge arguments lately. So after we finished praying for them, I asked them about it. The guy told me, "no, we never argue", but then the woman told me that they never used to argue, but that they had been arguing a lot within the past week. She also said that the night before they had a really big argument. She then asked me how I knew that. I told her that it was God that revealed it to me. They were amazed, and while I had their attention, I figured I'd tell them the rest of what the Holy Spirit told me. I then said to them, "the Lord said that these arguments are just the beginning. They are going to get worse, the longer you stay living in sin together and unmarried." The woman then looked at the guy and said, "I told you". I then looked at him and he said that they had talked about getting married but he wasn't sure about it. Dorian began to grill him with questions about why he didn't want to marry her to the point where he said, "I think I'm going to do it at the court house". I then repeated what the Lord had told me and told them that it would not get better, only worse. We prayed for them again and then we left.

10

AUGUST

August was the shortest month that I had as far as the number of people I witnessed to. On Saturday August 4th, I went to Northland Mall again to witness and talked to this guy named Donald. He told me that he was living a sinful life. He also told me that he was wanted for a crime and that he was going to turn himself in to authorities on that following Monday. He told me that he was being charged with three different crimes and that he was facing up to 30 years in prison. I ministered to him and told him how much God loved him. I also told him that he needed to come to church to get prayer for a miracle on his situation. He told me that he would come that next day, which was a Sunday. I followed him to his car to meet a woman that he had told me he had been dating. When I got to the car, I met a young lady named Briana, who was driving the vehicle. I then began to minister to her about their relationship and fornicating. I also ministered salvation to her and asked her about her walk with God. She told me that she wasn't saved. I then asked her if she and Donald could come to church tomorrow, and she said, "Yeah". I then told her to make sure that he came, and she said, "Alright, I will. We will be there". I then offered the both of them prayer and she exited her vehicle in the middle of the lane while the vehicle was still running and allowed me to pray for them. The next day, Donald and Briana came to church. Pastor Reggie prayed for them and prophesied over Donald's life. After church, Donald left and said his goodbyes with hopes of not seeing any of us again for a while. I talked to him several months after that and he told me that he never spent a day in jail. He said that the police gave him a tether to wear, but they still allow him to go to church if he wanted to, but he can't go anywhere else. He also stated that the police dropped two of the charges and only charged him with one. Also, there were eight other guys that were to stand trial with him, and they were all found guilty and are currently still in prison serving that time. When I talked to him, he was very thankful and just kept saying that he loved God and that he knew God was real. I asked him about his current walk with God and he said, "It's not going too bad, I mean I can't do too much wrong, I'm on house arrest." He was basically telling me that he was only living righteous because there was no hard sin around him to tempt him. You have to love God because of who He is, not based off of your current circumstances. You have to love God unconditionally, because the Lord doesn't put conditions on His love for us. People love God when they are up in life and hate Him when they are down or going through a troubling time in their life. People praise God when things are going good, but as soon as something changes for the worse, they are just as quick to deny him and doubt him. We are to love God because he first loved us! **(1 John 4:19)** We are to love and trust God despite our circumstances and the tests and trials that we endure. What if Jesus gave up on us? What if He said, "I'm not going and dying on that cross for these sinners", where would be today? The bible tells us to **"Trust in the Lord with all your heart, and lean not on your own understanding"** –Proverbs **3:5.** We have to give everything over to Him. Every bill, every debt, every struggle, every hurt, every sickness, every job, and even all anger, give it all to Jesus. Don't try and understand how you are going to pay your bills because you missed a whole week of work, trust in the Lord. Don't try and figure out how you are going to provide for your family because you just lost your job last week, trust in the Lord. Don't try to understand how God works. God is omnipotent (all powerful), omniscience (all knowing), and omnipresent (present everywhere). Don't sweat about anything worldly because God has given his son, Jesus, all authority in Heaven and on Earth. **(Matthew 28:18)**

On August 23rd, my family and I went on a cruise. Nicole couldn't go because she had to work and couldn't take off. No, I didn't want to leave my wife, but we had already prepaid for this trip and couldn't get a refund, so I reluctantly went. We car pooled down to Florida where the cruise was set to depart from. I prayed and asked God to still provide opportunities for me to minister while we were driving to Florida. I knew that once I got on the cruise that I was going to have many people to minster to. On the way down south, we stopped at several gas stations which afforded me the opportunity to minister to multiple people. When we arrived in Georgia on August 24th, we went shopping at Walmart. While I was there, I got hungry. I saw a McDonalds, but told myself that I would go somewhere else and get something to eat. The Lord told me to go to that McDonalds and eat. I didn't know why he told me this, but I complied and went. After paying for and receiving my food, I went over to the soda machine to fill up my cup. While I was over there, I saw this guy who had a mean look on his face sitting down eating. The Lord told me to minister to him. I went over to the guy and asked him about how his food tasted and he replied, "straight". I then said, "God is good man, and he's going to bless my food" and he replied, "I know that's right", and I was in. I began to minister to him and he told me that he believed in God, but was struggling trusting in Him because he was unemployed. I told him that the bible says to **"call on God, and He will answer you, and show you great and mighty things, which you do not know"** –Jeremiah 33:3. I then told him that once he gets saved and accepts Jesus Christ into his life, that he receives God's inheritance. You then will be able to call on God and He will help him in the best way possible. If you fall and scrape your knee, your parents come and dust you off, kiss it, and provide first aide for you. They do whatever it takes to make you stop crying, and you feel at peace because they cared for you, even though the pain and scar are still there. It's the same with God, just call on Him and when He comes, He brings you His peace that surpasses all understanding. **(Philippians 4:7)** Even though you are still in the fire and hurting and have the same circumstances, now you are content in those circumstances. He listened to everything I said while still eating his food. I actually waited until he got finished eating and then prayed for him.

On the cruise, it was harder than I thought to witness to people. While there were many people on the cruise, everyone was focused on having fun, not trying to hear about Jesus. I had to use tactics and be real sensitive to the Holy Spirit. On August 27th, I ministered to this older guy named Anthony. He told me that he was Catholic, but didn't really believe in Catholicism. He then went on to tell me about a car accident that occurred while he was on his way to the cruise. He told me that he and his family were on their way to Florida when their car flipped over. He told me that it was him, his wife, and his two sons. He told me that the car was totaled, but they all came out unharmed. He told me that Mary didn't do that, but it was Jesus that kept him and his family safe. He then told me that while he was at the hospital, his heart rate was high and they wanted to keep him there. He said, he told the nurse that he had to get to Florida to go on the cruise. He said that he and his family began to pray and that God made a way for them to be there on the cruise. He told me that he grew up a Catholic and raised his kids as Catholics, and that it was just a 'family thing'. I told him that he needed to serve a true God in a true faith that he completely believed in. He told me that he had already been talking about it with his family. People tell me a lot that they are saved and going to Heaven just because they have been in church since they were kids. You can't make it to Heaven based off of your parent's salvation. When it comes to entering into Heaven, no one can pray you through, except Jesus, who is our intercessor. On August 30th, I was sitting at the bar drinking a soda when this young lady sat down and ordered an alcoholic beverage. She then looked at me and started talking to me about the cruise. She told me that she was there with her church and I stopped and looked at her. I asked her about her salvation and why she was drinking. She told me that she was saved, but still had to work on drinking. She then asked me if one drink was wrong, and then I asked her, "Is you killing only one person wrong?" She laughed and said, "I guess so". I began ministering to her and told her that the bible says to **"be sober and vigilant"** – 1 Peter 5:8. I then told her that if you give the Enemy an inch, he is going to take a mile. You should not give the Devil any reign over you, because he will take it and run with it. She then told me the famous line, "Jesus turned water into wine". This is a perfect example of people taking biblical scripture and twisting it to support their sinful acts. I believe Jesus turned the water into wine because His mother asked Him to and He wanted to follow the commandment to "honor thy mother and father" **(Deuteronomy 5:16)**. Also the wine that was drank back in Jesus' day was different then today's wine, but that's a whole different story. This didn't even apply to her situation though, because she was drinking hard liquor. She listened to what I had to say and then poured the drink out. Please don't be deceived by the Devil's tricks. Do not tamper with **any** type of alcoholic beverage with the belief that you will only drink a little or that you are strong, and it is not possible to get drunk.

11

On September 6th, I ministered to a very unique individual. This was another guy that I have known since I was a kid. He was currently an Elder at a church. Ever since I have known him, he has been a heavy drinking alcoholic and fornicated with prostitutes. He told me that he had just recently become an Elder. I began to talk with him about his current walk with God and he told me that he was still saved. I then asked him about the drinking, and he told me "Ain't nothing wrong with a little drink every once in a while". He was in a leadership position at his church, which means that he is supposed to minister and talk to other people struggling with drunkenness. How can you minister to or help someone with drinking if you need help with it yourself? **(Matthew 7:2-5)** I ministered to him and then asked him about the prostituting. He told me that he was only having sex with one prostitute and he planned on marrying her. He then told me that she didn't want to marry him, but he was going to keep trying. Meanwhile he asked me, "Do you have any girls to hook me up with so I can leave her alone?" This guy was an Elder of a church and living a filthy and dishonorable lifestyle. As I stated earlier, he has been attending this same church and living like this since I was a kid. Now I was grown, and the Devil still was moving in his life. I continued to minister to him, but the more I ministered, the more excuses he gave me. The scary part about the whole conversation is that he never admitted that he was sinning or even showed conviction. I still pray hard for this man every day.

On September 14th, I ministered to one of my female cousins who proclaimed to be a homosexual. She told me that she liked women because men have done her wrong and that "all men were dogs". She told me that women knew how to treat her. She also told me that she wasn't saved, but was visiting a church occasionally. This world is now filled with people who accept homosexuality. I will never accept homosexuality as a man of God. There are churches that are afraid to preach against this subject in fear of losing some members. Some people will leave a church because a certain type of word is being preached and that word is convicting their heart. As I stated earlier, conviction means that the Holy Spirit is dealing with you and not allowing you to get complacent in your sin. When you stop feeling convicted, you are in trouble and need some spiritual guidance quickly. I began to minister to her and tell her about homosexuality. She listened and asked questions. She asked me, "doesn't God love everyone?" I told her, "yes" but at the same time everyone is not going to Heaven, only the righteous will enter into His kingdom." God destroyed Sodom and Gomorrah due to homosexuality, so how much more will he destroy one person. I told her that it is not God's intention though and that the bible says that He wants everyone to be saved. (2 Peter 3:9) I further told her that He is constantly knocking on the door of her heart, asking her to come in and dine with her. (Revelations 3:20) Homosexuality is wicked and has been that way since the beginning of Creation. God created Adam and Eve, not Adam and Adam, or Eve and Eve. The bible says that "a man and woman shall become one flesh -Genesis 2:24, Mark 10:8). I told her that a woman cannot do for her what a man can do for her and vice versa. We were all born with an automatic desire for the opposite sex, that's how God created us. There is no such thing as being born as a homosexual. The Lord said, "before you were born I sanctified you" – Jeremiah 1:5, which means that as a baby you were sanctified and holy. Now as a child, you can adopt these actions/desires from other people/spirits and things that you observe around you, but you don't come out of your mother's womb with a desire for the same sex. She told me that she was going to visit my church and till this day, I still await with negative results. But 'I planted the seed'.

On September 19ᵗʰ, I stopped at McDonalds to get something to eat. I had just left court and hadn't eaten anything all morning and was starving. As I was walking to the McDonalds entrance, this homeless man approached me and asked me for some money to buy some food. As for me, I rarely give homeless people money. A lot of them struggle with addiction and I don't want to support their habit or sin. If I talk to them and minister to them and am led by the Holy Spirit, I will bless them with some money. If they ask for food, I'll buy them food, but not before ministering to them. Homeless people need that attention just to let them know that there are people in this world that still cares for them. They are still human and have a heart, and based off my experience most of them feel lonely a lot of the times. He told me that he used to be saved, but then lost faith due to his circumstances. I then asked him, "is not the same God that you had faith in when you had material things, the same God of today?" He said, "I guess so, but it can't be". I gave him the scripture, **"Jesus Christ *is* the same yesterday, today, and forever –Hebrews 13:8.** I told him that God never changes, people and their situations do. I then told him that he needed to be content in his current situation and trust in God who is still with him. **(Philippians 4:11)** I then told him that I knew it sounded easier than it looked, but that I also had been in bad predicaments where I had it bad and had no food and almost lost my home. He asked me how I did it, and I told him, "I kept my faith". I then explained to him that if he expected God to deliver him out of his situation that he had to be saved and live righteous. **"Many are the afflictions of the righteous, but the Lord delivers them out of them all" –Psalms 34:19.** God hears the cries of the righteous and answers our prayers. **"The righteous cry, and the Lord hears, and delivers** them out of all their troubles" –Psalms 34:17. I then told him that he couldn't keep asking people for money and trusting them to set him free from his situation, but he had to trust in the Lord to set him free. **"Blessed is the man who trusts in the LORD, and whose hope is the LORD" –Jeremiah 17:7.** He then asked me if he had to stop begging for money, and I told him that he didn't have to stop doing it, but just don't make it your 'god'. He told me that he loved God and never wants God to give up on him. I prayed for him and went inside the McDonalds and bought him some food and gave it to him.

Some of us as believers also struggle with this same problem of worrying. Jesus Christ went to the cross to deliver us from all sin and with his death we were loosed from the chains of enslavement. So why do we sweat the small stuff? We are forever indebted to Jesus. Why are we worrying about how we are going to pay the rent instead of worrying about how to pay on our debt to Jesus? We have to understand that what we can't afford or what our money can't buy, grace will give it to us. When your children come up to you and ask for lunch money, they don't know how you are going to get it or where it's coming from, they just trust that you have it and will provide it for them. We have to come to God the same way, not knowing how He is going to provide, but trusting that He will. The next day, while I was at court I talked to this guy named Antwan. He told me that he was saved, but still went out to clubs to party and get drunk. I asked him, "if you were to have died yesterday, where would you be today, Heaven or Hell?" he replied Hell. I then told him that he contradicted himself and asked him if he knew what being saved meant. I then explained the meaning of being saved and salvation to him. I then asked him if he knew what Hell was, and he told me that it is a place where you burn. My personal analysis that I have gathered through my experience is that one of the biggest reasons why people sin is because they don't know what Hell truly is and what it has in store for them. The bible says that in Hell there is an unquenchable fire (**Mark 9:43**), it is a place of weeping and gnashing of teeth (**Matthew 13:42**), and that you will be tormented day and night, forever and ever **(Revelations 20:10)**. The scariest part about Hell is that you will be forever separated from God **(2 Thessalonians 1:9)**. These people will be punished with everlasting destruction and shut out from the presence of the Lord and from the glory of his might forever. It is scary to never have God's mercy or love ever again. I explained all this to him and he said, "Well I don't think I want to go there". I then told him that it's based on his personal relationship with Jesus Christ and his lifestyle. He then told me, "I don't do too much wrong". I said, "there are people who are living every day of their lives unto God and will barely make it into Heaven, so what do you think will happen to a person struggling with sin". **(1 Peter 4:18)** He looked at me and his eyes began to tear up. I told him that I didn't want him to be sad or afraid, because in Jesus Christ there is hope. He thanked me for the advice and went into the courtroom.

On September 24th, I had car trouble and went to my personal mechanic. While I was up there getting my car repaired, I had an opportunity to witness to this guy who worked there named Eric. He was up there with two of his friends. As I stated earlier, witnessing sometimes is about timing, you have to wait on the Lord. Sometimes we want to go outside of God's will and minister on our own, but what you might to do is say the wrong thing and ruin your opportunity to have an effect on winning that person over to Christ . I have been up to this mechanic shop many times before, and have seen Eric many of times, but never ministered to him because I wasn't led by the Holy Spirit. This time I was led by the Lord to minister to him and his friends. The Lord will give you certain tactics on how and when to minister. Once you've been doing it for a while, you will know when to jump into a conversation and start talking about the Lord. On this particular occasion, these guys started asking me questions about the law and my job. I responded to most of their questions, but then deferred with "the Lord keeps me safe on my job", and that was my entry point on bringing God into the conversation. They listened and tried to go back to me, but I kept the conversation on Jesus. These were some guys who have done a lot of very sinful things in their lives and needed Jesus, just like I once needed Jesus, and still need Him. I ministered to them and invited them all to church the next day, and they all said that they would come. I called Eric the next morning and he told me that he didn't need a ride because his friends were going to bring him to church. I called him about an hour before church was to start and he told me that he was on his way. Church started and he was not there. I called him after church and he told me that his friends took him somewhere else. When people make up in their mind that they are going to go to church, the Devil is going to try everything possible to keep them from going. He makes them extra tired Sunday morning, or makes them have car trouble, or makes someone call them with a problem, etc., this is how the Devil works. He knows that the Word of God is powerful, so it is his job to keep that Word away from sinners **and** saints. When ministering to someone and inviting them to church, if they accept the invitation, I always tell them to expect unforeseen challenges that will try to keep them from coming.

In the beginning of September, I received a flyer from Dodge dealership that said that I won some money and that I had a certain amount of time to respond to the flyer to receive it. I put it off due to the fact that I have received many of these types of flyers in the mail and they always ended up being bogus. On the morning of September 28th, I was praying in my car and I found the flyer. I then went to the Dodge dealership to see what it was all about. When I got there, I talked to this guy named Ron Walters. He started talking to me about the flyer and said that I didn't really win anything. While he was talking to me I could feel the Spirit of God all over him. So I mentioned God to him and he told me that he was saved. He told me that he was from Alabama and up here in Michigan just for a short time to handle the promotions on the flyers. He then told me that he was going back to Alabama Sunday night. He told me that he wanted to go to church that following Sunday, but didn't know where to go. I invited him to my church and he obliged. He told me that he needed a ride and I told him that I would gladly pick him up. When Sunday September 30th came, I went to go and pick him up at the hotel that he was staying at. When I arrived, he was standing outside waiting and ready to go and receive the Word. While we were driving to church, he began to tell me how he used to be married, but divorced his wife. He said that the Lord helped him find a new woman whom he was now engaged to. I ministered to him about his situation and just told him to trust in the Lord. Sometimes things happen in our lives and we don't understand why they happen. All you can do is trust in the Lord and pray that His will and purpose be done in the situation. **"All things work together for good to them that love God, and to them who are called according to *His* purpose" – Romans 8:28.** This scripture said that **all** things. So if you love God, just know that whatever you are going through, whether good or bad is going to work out for your good. It all was ordained by God before you were born. **(Psalms 37:23)** He then told me that he was a gospel music artist/producer and trusting in God to assist him in his career goals. We made it to church and afterward, he told me that he really enjoyed the service. On the way back to his hotel, we stopped at a gas station and we began to minister to this guy named Ray that was sitting on a motorcycle smoking. Ray told us, "Man I'm too old to be trying to get saved". I told him that Jesus came so that we may have life, and have it more abundantly. **(John 10:10)** I then told him that you can receive salvation at any age. **"For as in Adam all die, even so in Christ all shall be made alive" – I Corinthians 15:22.** It was through Adam that sin and death entered into the world, but through Jesus, we were all given a "new life" or a second chance. We continued ministering to him and prayed for him. When we got finished praying for him, the Lord led Ron to pray for a woman that was standing next to our gas pump watching the whole thing. Ron told her that he wanted to pray for healing in her body. Then she said, "Yeah I need a healing, how did you know that?" Ron told her that it was the Holy Spirit. We prayed for her and then left. Ron was definitely a man after God's own heart. He also had a great singing voice and was in the process of making a gospel cd. I am glad I had the opportunity to meet him. He definitely inspired me.

12

OCTOBER

As the end of the year drew closer and as I drew closer to my goal, things began to get harder. The enemy began to put other things/obstacles in my way that prohibited me from witnessing throughout the day. I found myself making excuses just to leave the house and go to the store and minister to someone. Once again, I really appreciate Nicole for having my back and having an understanding heart for my goal. She wasn't always happy about me leaving the house late at night, but she understood the purpose. On October 4th, I left the house around 9:30 pm to go to Meijer and minister to someone. While I was driving there, my fuel light came on in my car, so I stopped at a gas station. When I stopped there, I went into the gas station and saw these two young guys in there. I paid for my gas and left out the station. While I was pumping my gas, the two young guys came outside. I approached them and began to talk to them. They both had real foul mouths and were cursing a lot and just seemed angry at the world. I began to talk to them about Jesus and there language toward me changed and became less vile. (As I stated earlier, the Holy Spirit will change the atmosphere). One of the guys named Aaron told me, "I'm not ready to live for God, because I'm young. I got my whole life ahead of me to live for God, but for now I want to have fun". Now me being a police officer and seeing young kids killed all the time, I knew for a fact that this wasn't true. I told him that 'this life' is not guaranteed. People die every day with that same mindset of thinking that they have a long life ahead of them. You never know when your life is going to end. You also never know when the world is going to end. The day of the Lord will come as a thief in the night and the earth will be destroyed. **(2 peter 3:10)** Remember in 2011 when the Twin Towers and multiple other targets were attacked by terrorists, people all over the country ran into the churches and filled them up, because people thought that the end of the world was here. I then told him that many people, especially 'us' as men, try to organize our lives ourselves, and serve God when we're older and feel like everything is in order. But that's incorrect, the bible tells us to **"First seek the kingdom of God, and his righteousness; and all these things shall be added unto you" –Matthew 6:33.** He asked me if being saved would ruin all of his fun, and I told him that living for God would bring him even more joy and happiness in his life. His friend really didn't say too much except that he wasn't saved, but didn't know why. I asked them if I could pray for them and they obliged. As I was praying for them, a police officer pulled into the parking lot and went inside the store. I saw the gas station attendant pointing in our direction, and then several minutes later the police officer left the store and started walking towards us. He ignored the fact that we were praying and questioned the guys about harassing the gas station attendant. They denied it, so he asked me if I saw anything. I told him that they were respectful when I entered into the store, which was the truth. The police officer then told them that they had to leave and then he walked away. I then began finishing the prayer with them and the police officer walked back toward us and stated in a firm voice, "They have to leave now". Aaron replied, "Can we please finish our prayer?", and the officer didn't respond. I finished and closed out the prayer and they left the parking lot.

On October 7th, I stopped at the gas station after church and talked to this guy named Randy. After talking to him for a while he told me that he was living a sinful lifestyle. I asked him if he knew God, and he told me, "yeah". I then asked him if he knew God personally and he asked me what the difference was. I told him that he had to get to know God personally if he expected to receive anything from the Lord. I then told him, "I know President Obama, but I don't know him personally". So if I was to approach him and ask him for some money, I'm pretty sure he would look at me and say, "No, who are you". But if I knew him personally and we were friends and I asked him that same question, I might get a different response. The Lord is the same way, you can't come to God making request and expecting Him to work in your life and you don't personally know Him. The bible says that many people will come to God and feel that they deserve to enter Heaven, but He will say to them **"depart from Me, I never knew you"** – **Matthew 7:23.** He then told me, "The bible says that God is our friend in need. I told him that he was correct, but he couldn't serve two masters. **(Matthew 6:24)** You cannot be a friend to God and a friend to the World. Satan is the ruler of the World, so if you are friends with the world you are friends with Satan. He told me that he wasn't serving two masters, and that he didn't know God personally, but he still loved Him. I asked him, "How can you love someone that you don't know?" He then told me that he wanted to be saved and know God personally and asked me how he could receive salvation. I walked him through the prayer of repentance and he received salvation. Not even a week later, on October 13th, I ministered to another guy named Randy at the exact same gas station. I approached him and we started talking about God. He told me that he used to be saved, but he had been backsliding for a long time. He told me that he was living with his girlfriend and they had planned on getting married. I asked him, "If you were to have died yesterday, where you would be today, Heaven or Hell?" He replied Heaven. So I asked him on what account would he be able to say, "God let me into Heaven"? He told me, "I mean, I sin, but everybody does, I'm still saved". Salvation is a gift from the Lord. If someone gives you a gift and you give it back to them because you no longer want it, it's no longer your gift. He then went on and asked me, "don't you sin?" I told him, "yeah, but I still have to repent. I always ask for the Lord's forgiveness, for the sins that I have knowingly or unknowingly committed. Also, there is a difference between intentional/habitual sin and unintentional sin." We can unintentionally sin by unknowingly doing things that are displeasing to the Lord. When you are born again and living for God you are not to knowingly/intentionally sin. **(1 John 3:9)** Intentional sin is when you know it is wrong to do something and know the repercussions of God's judgment, but do it anyway. **"Therefore to him that knoweth to do good, and doeth it not, to him it is sin" – James 4:17. "For if we sin willfully after we have received the knowledge of the truth, there no longer remains a sacrifice for sins" – Hebrews 10:26**. He then started crying and told me that he was trying to live righteous and that he and his girlfriend had been looking for a church to attend. I comforted him and prayed for him. He rededicated his life back to Christ and I invited him to my church, which was right up the street about two blocks away. He said to me, "oh that's right up the street, I only stay around the corner. I shouldn't have any problem coming to your church". Till this day I still haven't seen him, but 'I planted the seed'.

October 16th was another one of those late nights where I had left the house pretty late to go to Meijer to minister to someone. I usually went to the Meijer close to our apartment, but for some reason, I just started driving and ended up at a different Meijer. When I got to Meijer, I parked my vehicle and saw five guys who worked at Meijer standing outside in the parking lot at a shopping cart corral talking. I went over there and began to talk to them. As soon as I mentioned Jesus, one of the workers walked off and went back inside the store. I began to minister to the remaining four, and inquiring about their walk with God. Only two of them were really responding to me and asking questions. After talking to them for several minutes about living righteous, one of the two told me that he knew God and knew about the Bible. So I asked him why he wasn't living righteous, and his response was, "because these girls out here be looking good and I got church in my heart, so I don't need to go to nobody church". I then stated, "Well you might have church in your heart, but you don't have God in your heart". He then looked at me, started walking away, and said that he would be back because he had to go and punch back in for work. Even though he said that he knew about God and Hell, I felt like I was probably too aggressive towards him. I felt that my words probably offended him and that he wasn't coming back out. I turned to the other guy who told me that he had no idea of what was sinful or not, and I showed him compassion. I am very bold when it comes to witnessing and pretty straightforward. I don't always minister Heaven or Hell to people. I am always led by the Holy Spirit and like I stated earlier, I use tactic to minister. If the Lord tells me to be bold, I'm bold, but if He tells me to be compassionate, I'm compassionate. The bible tells us to have compassion on some people when ministering, but on others save them with fear, hating the sin that contaminate their lives. **(Jude 1:22-23)** Some people need that strong and forceful word in their lives, because although living sinful, they have been pampered by other saints or leaders ever since they came into the faith of Jesus. And for that reason, they feel like they are doing enough to enter into Heaven. Those people will keep playing with God unless they hear the truth about Heaven and Hell and understand that it is not a joke. While on the other end, some people have a sensitive spirit and don't take well to aggressiveness. Also those same people may not even know about Jesus, never the less focused on Heaven or Hell. These kind of people need love and compassion. **"Therefore with lovingkindness have I drawn thee" –Jeremiah 31:3.** The bible also tells us that **"love will cover a multitude of sins" -1 Peter 4:8.** So while some people are stubborn and need fear to have the stubbornness broke, some people don't know God, but know that Jesus was about love, and expect that same kind of approach from you. The compassionate approach didn't work on me, so I was glad when Pastor Reggie preached Heaven or Hell in my presence. So, I continued ministering to the other guy who told me that he didn't know what sin was. He told me that he believed in God, but didn't know that it was wrong to drink, club, or fornicate. I told him some scriptures in the bible and gave him some knowledge on those things. I then told him that from that day forth if he continued to sin that he would be held accountable for those sins. **(Hebrews 10:26)** I told him that now he knew right from wrong. While I was talking to him, the guy who went to punch back in to work surprisingly walked back out there and said to me, "now what were you saying about me not having God in my heart?" I answered his question saying, "Do you have God in heart? Do you love God?" He responded, "Yeah, I love God". I told him that if he loved God, he would follow his commandments. **(John 14:15)** He was an example of a person who had not only a sin issue, but a heart issue. People get saved and begin to have faith in God and think that is enough to make it into Heaven. When you get saved, you need to have a heart transformation **(Ezekiel 36:26)** and put the Word of God in your heart to begin and stay living righteous. **"For it is with your heart that you believe and are justified" –Romans 10:10. "Thy word have I hid in mine heart, that I might not sin against thee" –Psalms 119:11.** I then told him that he needs to commit to a church. I don't believe in staying at home every Sunday watching church on TV, unless you are unable to maneuver around and go to a church. You need to be in the presence of other saints. **(Hebrews 10:25)** The church needs you, and you need the church. You are forsaking the kingdom of your gifts when you stay at home away from church. Your gifts are for the edifying of the body of Christ. **(Ephesians 4:11)** A lot of people say that a church is just a building. This is true, but the saints are the body which make the church, and you need the church to get spiritually fed. If you were to go weeks without natural food, then your body will get weak and not function properly. The same thing goes with spiritual food. If you miss weeks of church, then your body won't get the adequate amount of spiritual food that it needs to repel sin. After telling him all this, he thanked me for being hard on him and "telling him like it is". He told me that no one had ever rebuked him, or told him that how he had been living was wrong. Both he and the other guy I talked to received salvation. The other two guys told me that they weren't ready to give their lives over to the Lord.

13

NOVEMBER

On November 6th, one of my very close friends, Pastor Linnie Swanigan and I were at Joe Dumars Fieldhouse playing basketball. While I was sitting on the bench, I saw this other younger guy sitting on the bench next to me getting dressed to leave the gym. I spoke to him and we started a conversation. During the conversation, he started cursing a lot. I asked him, "why are you cursing so much?", and he replied, "because I'm grown". I then asked him what was the purpose for that type of language and he replied, "this is just how I talk man, I'm grown". I then told him that I didn't talk like that and I was grown. I asked him if he was saved, and he told me, "I really don't go to church, but I do believe in Jesus". I then asked him about his lifestyle, and he told me that he lives life day by day. I asked him about his future, and what happens after he dies. He said, "I will worry about that when it gets here". I began ministering to him and letting him know who Jesus really is. I told him that he had to stop with that language if he wanted to live for Jesus and develop a personal relationship with Him. People feel like cursing is small and not really sinning, but it is. The bible says, **"but as He who called you is holy, you also be holy in all your conduct, because it is written, 'Be holy, for I am holy'"-1 Peter 1:15-16.** Cursing is not edifying to the body of Christ, so it is something that is sinful. **"Let no corrupt word proceed out of your mouth, but what is good for**

necessary edification, that it may impart grace to the hearers" – **Ephesians 4:29.** Cursing is looked upon as negative and bad, which means that us as Christians shouldn't do it. As Christians, we are supposed to refrain from all appearances of evil or wrongdoing. **(1 Thessalonians 5:22)** Linnie came and sat down and already knew what I was talking to him about. Linnie told him that if he wanted to be saved and live for God that he had to change his heart. He told him, "God loves you, but he wants you to love him back. But not with your mouth or words, but with your heart and actions." The guy said, "I think I can do that". He then packed up all his stuff and left the gym. I really thank God for Linnie. I have ministered to several people with him, and he always ministers 'love' and people really relate to and comprehend him and his message. This was another example of the many opportunities that we as Christians have to minister to people. Here we were at a gym playing basketball and enjoying leisure activities, but the Lord still led us to minister to someone.

On November 9th, Dorian and I had plans to go to Northland Mall to witness. This day was the best overall experience that we had together while out witnessing. As I was getting ready to leave home and head to the mall, I had cut my finger on a can of food while trying to open it. My finger started bleeding nonstop. I had poured water and alcohol on it, but it kept bleeding. I then tried putting multiple Band-Aids on the cut, but the blood leaked through them. Finally after about 20 minutes, the bleeding had begun to lighten up, and I left to head to the mall even though I was now running late. The Devil will try and stop you from doing the work of the Lord, but you have to press your way through his evil barriers. As I stated earlier, the Apostle Paul had many shipwrecks while on journeys to spread the gospel of Jesus, but he continued and pressed his way forward. **(Philippians 3:14)** When I first made it to the mall, my finger had started bleeding profusely again. Dorian met me outside in the parking lot with some peroxide to try and stop the bleeding, but the peroxide didn't stop it. I just wrapped my finger up with napkins and we headed toward the mall. When we entered the mall, we prayed before we started like we always did. When we finished praying, my finger stopped bleeding. I put one last Band-Aid on the cut and we began to minister to people. The first guy that we encountered name was Dom, who was with his friend. Both of these guys were young, but Dom's friend was very immature and kept laughing and trying to get Dom to walk away. We began to talk to Dom about his lifestyle. He told us, "I sin, but I don't break any major sins". I told him that the bible says **"For whoever shall keep the whole law, and yet stumble at one point, he is guilty of all" –James 2:10.** He asked us if he was going to Hell for sinning, and I told him, "that is where it leads you, but there is hope in Jesus, who paid the price for that sin". He then asked, "Why Hell, I mean I only break small sins?" I then told him that sin is sin, and we all deserve death. Hell is the punishment for those sins. It is only the blood of Jesus Christ that cleanses us. Then I told him that Dorian and I both will also get judged and that the bible says that judging will start with the saints first. **(1 Peter 4:17)** He then said, "but I'm a good person". I told him "God has to judge sin. Let's say you commit a lot of crimes, get arrested, and stand before a judge. The judge says, 'before I sentence you is there anything else you would like to say?' and you respond with, 'well, I'm a good person and have just been going through a lot, this will never happen again'. The judge is still going to judge your crimes and sentence you accordingly, if he doesn't, he isn't a just judge." God is the same way, He is a just judge, and He is our Judge. **(Psalms 7:11)** Dorian then told him that he had to walk upright and that if he believed in his heart that Jesus was Lord then he needed to repent and give his life to God. He confessed his sins and received salvation. We started shouting, "Hallelujah!!! Glory to God! The bible says that angels in Heaven rejoice when a sinner repents. **(Luke 15:10)**

We continued on and encountered a young guy by the name of Jodie who had approached us and offered us some free jewelry cleaning. Dorian told him that we were fine and asked him if he was saved, he responded, "I'm a Muslim". So as we began to witness to him and question him about his faith, we found out that he knew nothing about Islam. Dorian then asked him, "Why are you a Muslim?" He responded, "because someone told me that the bible is fake". This 16 year old boy called himself a Muslim just because someone told him that Islam was the only real religion. We began to minister to him, and after probing through his life and childhood, we discovered that he had a rough childhood. He said that his parents were not saved and also not currently involved in his life, and he was living out of hotel rooms. This is a perfect example of **Proverbs 22:6- "Train up a child in the way he should go: and when he is old, he will not depart from it".** This young man had no parental supervision and no Godly role models. He asked us questions and we answered them for him. We continued to minister to him, but he didn't take us serious. We still did our part in giving him the gospel of Jesus Christ and opening his eyes up to the Holy Bible and to who Jesus is. At that time, we had been at the mall for about 2 hours and we were getting ready to leave. As we were walking toward the exit, Dorian noticed a lady that used to go to our church. He stopped and asked her how she and her family were doing. She stated that everything was good and that her husband was there with her walking around the mall somewhere. Dorian ended the conversation and we continued walking toward the exit. As we approached the mall exit, Dorian stopped and said that he wanted to see the young lady's husband and talk to him to catch up with him. So we turned around and began to walk back through the mall looking for this guy. As we were walking, we saw a lady named Lila walking with another lady, her mother. Lila was walking with a limp and her arm was in a bent cringed position against her chest. As I got closer, I noticed that her fingers were also stuck closed in a fist-like nature. Dorian asked her if we could pray for her, and she obliged. We asked if she was saved and if she believed in Jesus Christ and the power of healing, and she stated that she was saved and also filled with the Holy Spirit. I asked her what was wrong with her body, and she said that she had an aneurism in her right leg that paralyzed the whole right side of her body. I asked her to try and lower her arm and open her fingers. She attempted to, but her bones and muscles would not allow her to succeed. I then grabbed a hold of her arm and fingers to see how much force was restricting her from moving freely, and her muscles were indeed much tightened. We then began to pray, pray, and pray and quote healing scriptures. We were praying for about ten minutes and still nothing had happened, but we had faith. The bible says, **"It shall come to pass that before they call, I will answer; and while they are still speaking, I will hear" –Isaiah 65:24.** People from the mall had gathered around and had stopped and were watching us as we continued to pray. Then immediately, the Holy Spirit began to show His power. As we continued praying, her fingers began to open up and her right arm began to lower to a normal position. Her healing was taking place. I asked her to join in with us speaking in her Heavenly language (tongues) and we continued to pray. She complied and joined in prayer with us. She then began to jump around, her fingers began to open more, and her arm also lowered even more. We stopped and asked her to do something that she couldn't do before. She then began to squat, bend, and jog in place. Her mother started crying and stated that she wasn't able to do that before. I then asked her how she felt, and she said, "I feel amazing". She told us that she hadn't been able to move like that since she had the aneurism. I began to minister to her and tell her that she had to walk in her healing. I noticed that she was still trying to reach for things by bending over and slouching down. I told her again that she had to walk in her healing; that God didn't make us imperfect, and that He wants us to be healed and whole **(Luke 13:10-13)**. The Holy Spirit revealed to me that she was just content and comfortable in her sickness, and that she was so used to being in that state, that is all she knew. I asked her about it, and she agreed. I advised her that she needed to do more things with her arm and hand; make them more active. She was very appreciative of all that God had done for her and we were grateful that the Lord had used us to demonstrate His miraculous power.

On November 13th, I was getting ready for work when Nicole asked me to stop at the grocery store on the way in. On my way to work, I stopped at this grocery store called Imperial Palace. When I entered into the grocery store, I saw a woman standing in the lobby and she stared at me with a blank stare as I walked inside the store. I went inside the store for about 10-15 minutes. When I came out of the store, that same lady approached me and told me that she was selling some of her music. I asked her what kind of music it was, and she said, "it's gospel music". Now this grocery store was in one of the worse parts of Detroit as far as criminal activity. So the audacity of her to even be out there late at night selling music period, nevertheless gospel music was a shock to me. Up until that point, I had never encountered anyone that was selling/promoting their own gospel music on the street, everyone was always promoting their own rap music. She also told me that she was selling a book that she had just written. I asked her how much she wanted for the cd and book, and she replied, "I'm just taking donations, whatever you got". I checked my pockets and told her that I didn't have any cash on me, but that I had some money in my car. She said, "that's alright, I don't know you like that to be following you to your car". I told her that I was a police officer and didn't mean her any harm. I also went on and told her that I was saved, sanctified, and filled with the Holy Spirit. After saying that, she complied and followed me to my car. While walking to my car, I began asking her about her salvation and her relationship with God. She told me that she was saved, but that she needed prayer. I guess she could feel my anointing, because she repeatedly kept asking me for prayer. I asked her what she needed prayer for and she told me, "strength". First I went in my car and gave her money for the cd. Then I began to pray for her. While praying for her, the Holy Spirit began to give me revelation on a lot of things that she had been through in her childhood years and gave me something to tell her. I told her "God says that, 'He is mending your broken heart from your past and starting you off new. He is restoring you to a strong and mighty woman of God'." She began crying as I closed out the prayer. I asked her why she was crying so hard and she told me, "because I been through a lot in my life and this is why God had me write this book. I am struggling to keep my faith because of my life". I then began to ask her about the things the Lord showed me about her childhood and she confirmed these things. She then started crying harder and the Lord gave me a word for her and I told her, "God said 'just believe'." She then grabbed me and hugged me and started crying even harder. I stopped her and asked her what was wrong. She reached inside her coat pocket and pulled out a cd that was titled 'Just Believe'. She then stated, "That is the title of my new cd that I just wrote two weeks ago". I prayed for her some more and gave her the scripture **(2 Timothy 1:7) - "For God has not given us the spirit of fear; but of power, and of love, and of a sound mind".** I then told her that she needs to have peace and a sound mind in her life and that she had the power to trample over the enemy **(Luke 10:19)**, instead of letting the enemy put fear into her life. I invited her to church and continued on to work. The whole way to work, I just kept thinking to myself, "what if Nicole didn't send me to the grocery store to get some food?"

On November 27th, I was working and encountered a guy at the hospital whose uncle had just died. He was emotionally distraught over the death and crying, but he was also causing a loud disturbance. I walked over to him and told him that he had to calm down and he became aggressive, squared up, and wanted to fight. I asked him what was wrong with him, and he replied, "Don't nobody care about me, I'm all alone in this world". I asked him if he believed in Jesus and he told me that he somewhat did. I then questioned him further about his faith and he kept answering me aggressively. After several minutes of conversing, he told me to back up and leave him alone. He then started crying again and talking about how he didn't want to live anymore. I approached him again and said, "Look man you are loved, I love you". Other police officers began to look at me weird, but they didn't understand. He said, "You don't love me, you don't even know me." I was referring to the Godly love that I had for him. I then asked him if he loved God, and he told me, "yeah, but I ain't never seen him", and I replied, "Exactly". The bible tells us that in order to love God, you have to love your brothers. **"If someone says, 'I love God,' and hates his brother, he is a liar; for he who does**

not love his brother whom he has seen, how can he love God whom he has not seen?" -1 John 4:20. He looked at me with a blank stare and just said, "Thanks man, I really needed to hear that." We need to have love for our brothers and sisters in Christ, but also for the sinners. Jesus said, **"Those who are well have no need of a physician, but those who are sick" –Luke 5:31.**

We have to get to the point where we go outside of our comfort zones and the confinement of the four walls of the church and save those souls that need to be 'inside' the church. There is nothing wrong with being saved and preaching/hearing the gospel in church every Sunday, but we need to get the sinners into the church to hear about Jesus, and a lot of these sinners need to know that they are loved. They need to know that they can come to the house of God just as they are. The man that I mentioned earlier from the dry cleaners named Tyrone, who had high blood pressure came to my church one Sunday. He began to act out and became loud and obnoxious. I wasn't ashamed of the way he acted. It was my job to get him to the house of God and let him hear the word of God. If I would have brought a drunk to church, or a prostitute that was half-dressed, or even a drug addict, I still would not have been ashamed, because those are the ones that need the gospel. Should I be more impressed if I bring a saved man to church that is dressed in a nice suit, speaks well, is filled with the Holy Spirit, and speaks in tongue language? No I shouldn't, he has already been shown the path of life (**Psalms 16:11**), but the other people haven't.

14

On December 5th, I went to Meijer and saw this guy that worked there named Eric outside pushing baskets. I walked up to him and began talking to him about Jesus. I asked him if he was saved, and he told me that he was. I asked him how he knew he was saved, and he told me, "Because I believe in God". I then began to ask him about his lifestyle and he told me that he was living a sinful lifestyle. So I asked him, "how are you saved if you are living the way that you are living?" He replied, "We all are sinners, I just repent. I still believe in God, so I'm going to Heaven." I told him that it is more to it than just believing in God, and he replied, "You don't know what you talking about, the bible says that if I believe that God gave away his son Jesus to the world and believe in him that I'm going to Heaven." He was referring to the scripture **John 3:16 –"For God so loved the world that He gave His only begotten Son, that whoever believes in Him should not perish but have everlasting life."** I hear this scripture a lot while witnessing to people. Please don't be deceived. Just believing in God alone is not enough to make it into Heaven. The bible says that even the demons believe in God. **(James 2:19) John 3:16** says that you have to believe in Jesus. Jesus is the key to salvation. Jesus said**, "I am the way, the truth, and the life. No one comes to the Father except through me" – John 14:6.** Salvation is an ongoing process, not a one-time thing. You 'have' been saved from the penalty sin, you 'are' currently being saved from the power of sin, and you 'will' be saved from the presence of sin. You have to continuously repent and live according to His word after your initial confession of Christ. After that confession, you are saved and redeemed and adopted into the family of the Most High, but you have to continue to live a life that is acceptable and pleasing to God. He looked at me and told me that he was going to do some research on that. He still allowed me to pray for him and I invited him to church. On December 7th, I stopped at a store and encountered this guy named Clifford. He told me that he used to be saved. He also told me that he struggled with drinking because he was homeless and that drinking was how he coped with life. I asked him if he believed in Jesus, and he replied, "Yes, I used to". He told me that he wasn't in church because he was homeless. I told him that God loved him. People are so quick to give up on God when He doesn't come to their rescue immediately, or answer their prayers right away. I told Clifford that he needed to stop drinking his life away and playing the lottery in hopes of getting a 'big break'. The bible tells us to keep your lives free from the love of money and be content with what you have, because God will never leave you, nor forsake you. **(Hebrews 13:5)** I also told him that God rewards His people, but that he had to live right. I told him that he had to seek God diligently in order to get any of God's rewards. **(Hebrew 11:6)** He then told me that it was hard to live saved when you don't have much. I told him that the bible says that we should focus our minds on Heaven, not earthly things. **(Colossians 3:2)** I prayed for him and left the store.

Later that day, I had a chance to minister to a person who is very significant to my life, my dad, Dorian. He called me out of nowhere; I hadn't heard from him in a while. He told me that he was going to undergo surgery on his heart that following Monday, and that he just wanted to let me know. This wasn't the first surgery or big problem that he recently had with his body, but this was the most vital surgery. I have talked to my dad before about being saved and giving his life to Christ several times, but at that time I hadn't ministered to him in a while, so I did. I told him "all these problems are going to keep occurring until you give your life to Jesus", he replied, "I know". I told him that when he begins to live righteous that he will have the healing power of God at his aid. He asked me, "Can God really stop all these surgeries from happening?" I told him that the bible says, **"I have been young, and now I am old; yet I have never seen the righteous forsaken" –Psalms 37:25.** I told him that I will let the church know to add him to our prayer list. I also told him that he needed to come to church on Sunday. He told me that he would come, but when Sunday came he didn't answer his phone. I talked to him after the surgery and he told me, "It was God that helped me make it out of that surgery". He then told me he would come to church and change his life around. I continuously pray for my father.

At this time, the Lord had been putting it in my spirit to write this book. He kept telling me how to outline it and write it, but I never even thought about writing any book. On December 8th, I was at Linnie's house for a Christmas party, when I started talking to several people about my soul winning quest and about this possible book. Then this young lady come up to me and began to inquire about how she can minister on her job, or how to minister if you are shy. Then some other people asked me questions about ministering. This was confirmation from the Lord that this book was to be written not only to encourage saints, or save the lost, but to also be used as a guiding tool for ministering. The Lord will give/show you confirmation. On December 9th, I encountered a guy at the YMCA while I was playing basketball. This guy told me that he had a lust problem and felt that God put women on this earth for men to fornicate with. I told him that sexual intercourse was ordained by God for marriage. I further told him that all of his lust could lead him to Hell if he continued with it. He asked me, "Why should I stop looking at such a beautiful species?" I told him that he had to first get saved and give his life to God to understand why he couldn't fornicate or defile his body. I then told him that his eyes were the lamp of his whole body, and if they were good then his whole body will be good, but if they were bad, then his whole body will be filled with darkness and sin. (**Matthew 6:22**) He told me that he didn't understand what that meant, so I told him that his eyes causes his body to sin. He asked me why it was a sin to look at women bodies if he wasn't married. I told him that just looking is not a sin. The sinful part comes in when you look at their bodies in a lustful nature. The cycle first begins with temptations and desiring after a woman lustfully, then that desire gives birth to sin (sex), and then that sin brings forth death (Hell). (**James 1:14-15**) He looked at me and stated, "well I guess I have to stop doing that then, I didn't know it was that deep". I then told him, "that is how the Devil manipulates people minds, by their ignorance to the Word of God, and that's why it's important for you to be saved and study the bible on your own". He told me that he would and went back to playing basketball.

On December 19th, I was leaving Walmart when I saw a guy that I used to go to elementary school with. I approached him and we began to talk about our lives. I told him that I was saved and living for Jesus and asked him about his salvation. He told me that his faith was kind of wavering, but that he did believe in God. He told me that he had been through a lot of things in his life that caused him to question his faith in God. He began to go deeper into the occurrences that he was speaking of. He told me that he was engaged once and that his fiancée tried to kill him. He told me that when he looked her in the face, she looked demon possessed. She had physically harmed him to the point where he needed stiches and was in the hospital on life support, and almost died. I told him that the bible says that we don't fight against flesh and blood, but spiritual wickedness in high places. (**Ephesians 6:12**) He then told me that ever since then, he doubted God and His omnipotence. I told him that he had to be strong for

God and let God know that he can be trusted while in the fire. I then told him, "It is when you go through your trial and overcome evil that you are rewarded with a seat next to God's throne in Heaven". **(Revelation 3:21)** He began to tell me how her family wanted to kill him and how he contemplated getting revenge. I gave him the scripture **Romans 12:21 –"Do not be overcome by evil, but overcome evil with good".** He then told me that he believed it was God that kept him from hurting her back. He then asked me, "How did you know that your wife was right for you?" I told him, "It wasn't easy. I prayed and fasted hard and sought after God, and He answered." I told him that once you receive the Holy Spirit and develop a personal relationship with God, you begin to hear His voice very clearly. Many people say, "I can't hear God", or "God doesn't talk to me". God talks to us more often than we may think. The problem is that we can't hear Him because our hearts and minds are clotted with so much sin and garbage. Once you give your life to Jesus and begin to live for Him, you can have a personal conversation with Him, I do it often. God is a jealous God, and He wants all of you. Nothing in this world should come between you and your love for God. This guy was a perfect example. He told me that he used to cherish her and put her before everything. He also told me that she was the reason that he didn't go to church. You cannot let your spouse, children, parents, friends, family, pastors, or no one, come in between you and God. He told me that he wanted to be married and not fornicate, but he was scared to date another woman. I told him that he had to first seek God, and then God would do the rest. I told him that his salvation should be the most important thing in his life, not any woman. I prayed for him and he received salvation.

As the end of the year drew nearer, I grew stronger. The enemy tried to make me miss several days by throwing sicknesses my way, but I overcame and continued to press forward. On December 31st, I woke up and prayed for strength and courage to finish my quest. I also prayed that something miraculous would take place on this last day. I must have prayed for about an hour. Up until that day, I had not missed a day of witnessing, and said to myself that the person that I witnessed to that day was going to be so vital and crucial to my quest. I stayed at home most of the day, but went to Northland Mall to pick up some dry cleaning early that afternoon. When I went to the mall, I encountered these two young ladies and a guy that were walking together. I approached them and asked them about their salvation. The two young girls told me that they were living life and not really focused on God. I said, "not focused on God?" that's like not focusing on the air you breathing". They laughed and told me that they didn't mean it like that. Meanwhile, the guy told me, "all I'm worrying about living for is my son", at which time he pointed to a young boy that he was holding in his arms. I tried to probe deeper, but they kept telling me that they were in a hurry because it was New Year's Eve. So I asked them if I could pray for them and they complied. While I was praying for them, the Lord showed me so much about them, more than he has ever showed me about anyone before. After prayer, I turned to one of the girls and told her that she was un-employed and had been looking for a job, and she said, "That is right, how did you know that?" I then told her that she was ready to quit and give up on looking and she said, "Wow, yeah, I just told myself that I was going to give up and whatever happens, just happens". I told her that the Lord said, "hold on, a job is coming soon, keep your faith." I then turned to the other girl and asked her if she was dating a guy, and she told me that she was. I asked her if he was a very dark-skinned man, and she said, "Yes". I then asked her if he was a really tall skinny man with dreads, and she said, "Yea, wow, how did you know that? Who are you, this is creepy." I then told her that the Lord said, "this isn't the man for you, don't waste any more time with him." I didn't want to tell her this because I didn't know how she would take it, but I couldn't offend the Holy Spirit by not releasing what He told me to release. **"Do not quench the spirit" -1 Thessalonians 5:19.** After I told her that, she said, "that's crazy that you telling me this, because I was just contemplating breaking up with him, because he been acting stupid". I then went to the guy and said, "you and the baby mother have been arguing a lot, and she doesn't want to give you your son, does she?" He said, "yeah we been arguing, and she don't want me to see my son." I then said "and the family have been trying to cut you out of the picture and get rid of you for good, right?" He said, "yeah they have been, they real dirty." I then told him that God said, "You are a good father. Hold on to your son and don't let him go easy. He will work it out for you, things will get easier". He said, "Alright", and just looked at me with a strange look. At this time the two girls looked at me and told me that they were amazed at what had just happened and that I didn't know how much I impacted their lives. I then told them, "No, you don't know how much you all have impacted my life". I then told them about my quest and they said that it was 'cool'. Then out of nowhere, here comes the enemy trying to destroy the Word of the Lord that just went forth. The guy said, "Man I don't believe none of that". The two girls started getting upset and stating, "No, I believe it, I believe that. You don't know what you talking about, stuff like that is true, I believe him". I then told the girls to relax and told them that stuff like that happens, and that I wasn't offended. You will always have unbelievers and doubters, if we didn't, Jesus wouldn't have been put on the cross and killed. I asked him what he meant by his statement and he said, "Man anybody could of guessed that I had baby mama drama, what black man don't? You just guessed how her man looked and you lucked up and got it right, and how many people are unemployed in today's society." I replied to him, "oh ye of little faith. How did I know that you weren't a single parent, or married, or in a happy relationship with the baby's mother? How can I guess this guy's height, weight, skin complexion, and hairstyle correctly or know that she was thinking about breaking up with him? Even though unemployment is on the rise, the other girl is dressed well. There are many people out here that have good jobs, and I am one of them, and how did I know about her wanting to stop looking for a job?" He stood there with a disappointed look upon his face and told the girls, "Let's go y'all". Before they left, I invited them all to Watchnight service at my church that night and the two girls said that they wanted to go, but the guy didn't want to come. I told the two girls that I would come with another woman to pick them up if they wanted to come and they said, "Okay". That night came and I called the number that they gave me and received no answer. I went to Watchnight service and told the rest of the church that I completed my quest and they along with the angels in Heaven rejoiced.

15

AFTERMATH

So the end of the year finally came and I had completed my quest. It was hard and it was a struggle, but GOD IS GOOD! Since then, I have moved into a new house, my wife gave birth to our beautiful son, and I have witnessed to many, many more souls. Since I have been saved, new people have come into my life and old people have left my life. More people have left my life than those that have come in. You cannot count on people to stick around once you get saved. You have to be you! If that means being the only person in your 'circle', then so be it. You have to take a stand on sin, if not it will consume you. If you are holy, then be holy. If you are righteous, then be righteous, and not just in church, but also outside of the church. If you are a sinner, turn to Jesus. Jesus is the only one that can define your life; not your parents, spouse, teacher, pastor, friends, siblings, a woman or a man, but only Jesus. This world is filled with sin everywhere you look. This is a world full of sinners, and they definitely outnumber the righteous. That's why it is our goal to try and get them to join our side in the fight for righteousness. As Christians, we are always outnumbered. One thing that I appreciate about Jehovah Witnesses are that they go from door-to-door and spread 'their' gospel. It's the wrong gospel, but they still exhibit boldness. They also go out with their kids from door –to-door spreading their gospel. Us as Christians have to get more serious about our faith. We have to go outside of the comforts of our churches' four walls and minister to the lost that are outside the church. How many Jehovah Witnesses do you know that have been converted to Christianity? How many Muslims do you know that have been converted to Christianity? When was the last time you had someone come up to you talking about Jesus and trying to win you over to Christ? I can count on one hand since I have been saved how many people have approached me. Jesus told us to preach to all the nations, but we can't even preach to people in the same country, state, city, or even neighborhood. If you want better, you have to do better. Its timeout for passiveness and being lethargic when it comes to your faith. We have to get out here and spread the gospel of Jesus Christ to the world. How can someone believe in something if they never hear about it? **(Romans 10:14)**

16

PREPARING FOR BATTLE

I want everyone to understand that spreading the gospel of Jesus Christ is not going to be easy. Most people are not just sitting around waiting to hear about Jesus or Heaven; they would rather hear about the weather, or the news, or the newest shoes or fads. When it comes to spreading the gospel, you have to be prepared. The bible gives a detailed explanation on preparation. **Stand therefore, having girded your waist with truth, having put on the breastplate of righteousness, and having shod your feet with the preparation of the gospel of peace; above all, taking the shield of faith with which you will be able to quench all the fiery darts of the wicked one. And take the helmet of salvation, and the sword of the Spirit, which is the word of God; praying always with all prayer and supplication in the Spirit, being watchful to this end with all perseverance and supplication for all the saints – Ephesians 6:14-18**

We have to put in work for the Lord while down here on earth. We have to sow into the kingdom. If you are reading this book and think that you are going to Heaven based solely on the fact that you believe in and have faith in Jesus, but are living a sinful and displeasing lifestyle, then you need to check your salvation and reexamine yourself. Your faith is what justifies you, but your yielding to the will of God and holy lifestyle are what sanctifies you. Justification is an instantaneous occurrence when you confess Jesus Christ, with the result being eternal life. It is based completely and solely upon Jesus' sacrifice on the cross (1 Peter 2:24) and is received by faith alone (Ephesians 2:8). No works are necessary whatsoever to obtain justification. As I stated earlier, after your initial confession in Christ, you are to work on yielding more to the Holy Spirit to bring sanctification to yourself. Sanctification is the process of being set apart for God's work and being conformed to the image of Christ. This conforming to Christ involves the work of the person, but it is still God working in the believer to produce more of a Godly character and life in the person who has already been justified. Sanctification is not instantaneous because it is not the work of God alone, but it is a lifelong process of yielding to and being obedient to the Holy Spirit. During this process, you will daily grow a deeper relationship with the Lord and a strong desire to do His will. We have to continuously work on sanctifying ourselves. (Philippians 2:12)

I believe that faith without works is one of the most debatable topics of Christianity, at least based on most of my encounters with people. The bible says that **"faith without works is dead"** –James **2:17.** Faith produces good works; and works make faith perfect. Faith brings a person to salvation, and good works brings that person to faithfulness. The bible says that when you stand before God, He will say, "well done thy good and faithful servant". (**Matthew 25:21**) How can He say "well done" if you have done nothing to prove your faithfulness toward Him? Your faith has to produce good works. Works meaning: submitting to God's will, resisting sin, bearing 'fruit' (**Galatians 5:22-23**), ministering to others, living righteous, exemplifying a Christ-like lifestyle, etc. Do your earthly job through your good works so that your faith can be made perfect and you can offer up spiritual sacrifices acceptable to God through Jesus Christ. (**1 Peter 2:5**) If you truly believe in God and truly are a person after God's own heart, then your works will be demonstrated through your faith in Jesus. I'm not saying that works alone will get you a pass into

Heaven or that you can earn your way into Heaven. Salvation is a free gift and no one can stand before God and boast on their good works. The bible says, **"For by grace you have been saved through faith, and that not of yourselves; it is the gift of God, not of works, lest anyone should boast"** –Ephesians 2:8-9. A person who has true faith will have good works in their life. If a person claims to be a believer, but has no good works in their life, then that person most likely does not have genuine faith in Christ. If you have genuine faith and love for Jesus, then you have to follow His commands. The first command Jesus gave the apostles was to go out and minister the word of Jesus, and spread the gospel. **(Matthew 10:5-8)** God has given us the tools to minister, so why are we not using them? The bible says that we were created to do good works. **(Ephesians 2:10)** Jesus said, **"freely you have received, freely give"** –Matthew 10:8. It is a sin to withhold the knowledge of Jesus Christ and not share it with the lost. I'm sure many of you have heard the saying, "to whom much is given, much is required" **(Luke 12:48)**. Jesus said, **"I am the vine, you are the branches. He who abides in Me, and I in him, bears much fruit; for without Me you can do nothing"** –John 15:5. But if you do not bear fruit, the bible says that you are **"cast out as a branch and is withered; and they gather them and throw them into the fire, and they are burned** –John 15:6.

We have to use our tools to minister to the lost. If you are shy or meek and don't like talking to people, then let people see Christ through your Godly behavior. Don't get comfortable with this type of behavior though, because the bible says that **"though they are seeing they do not see, and hearing they do not hear, nor do they understand"** -Matthew 13:13. Also going to church every Sunday is not enough by itself to get you into Heaven. There are people that go to church every Sunday and are on their way to Hell. There are many hypocrites in churches that go to church on Sunday after partying in the club all night on Saturday. Jesus warns us about these people and tells us that they should be known by their fruits, or works. **(Matthew**

7:15-20) Salvation is not a CHURCH thing, but a HEART thing. The Lord looks at your heart more than your church attendance. Paul went to different nations ministering and spreading the gospel of Jesus Christ to different cultures and societies, yet us as Christians are afraid to minister to people of the same culture who sits right next to us at work. Your co-workers blast their ungodly music and curse up a storm around you, so why can't you open up your bible and brag on Jesus around them? Think about it! How many people reading this book right now can truly say that your friends and co-workers know that you are saved? There are so many Christians that are 'under-cover Christians', and that is wrong. Do not be ashamed of the gospel of Jesus Christ. **(Romans 1:16)** You have to be bold and represent for Christ. If I go to your friends and co-workers and ask them what kind of person you are, what would they say? Would they say, "Oh that's so & so, he's always laughing at my dirty jokes", or "oh that's so & so, she's always cursing and gossiping?" In doing this, you are causing that person to misperceive 'true Christianity' and true Christ-like characteristics. What good is it having the keys to the Kingdom of Heaven if you never use them? That's like having keys to a new car, but still catching the bus. Another famous saying is, "you can talk the talk, but can you walk the walk." We have to walk the walk, which means showing people what being a saved believer is really about. If you are battling with any strongholds, seek Godly counsel to assist you with it before allowing it to grow bigger and overtake you. . **"Therefore if the Son makes you free, you shall be free indeed"** –John 8:36. I believe once you are seen by a person committing a sin, your chances of drawing that person to Christ are slim.

God is calling for us to do more. His return is drawing nearer and the world isn't getting any nicer. Sin is becoming more prevalent and boastful. We have to speak out against it and not be ashamed of the end result or the persecution. The bible tells us to rejoice in this type of persecution. **(Matthew 5:11-12)** Do not be afraid to stand for holiness. Jesus said, **"But whoever denies Me before men,**

him I will also deny before My Father who is in Heaven" –Matthew 10:33. No more keeping our bibles in the car tucked away in the rear window, or using our bibles as paperweights. No more walking past homeless people or drug addicts and laughing at them instead of ministering to them. No more making it to work on time, but being late to church. No more complaining about church being too long, but working for 8 hours at your job or watching a 2-3 hour movie without complaining. No more keeping quiet when sin is amiss right in front of you, and the Devil is pointing at you laughing. It is time for a change, if not now, then when? If we want better, then we have to do better. As stated earlier, you have the keys to the Kingdom, now what are you going to do with them?

SALVATION

Living holy and doing the will of God isn't hard once you fall in love with Him and develop a personal relationship with Him. I get people that ask me all the time, "How do you do it?" or "What do you do for fun?" Once you develop a love for God, doing His work is what brings you joy. There were many days in the year of 2012 where I felt down or exhausted, but when I went out and ministered to someone, it brought joy to my heart and uplifted me. There are also worldly things to do that do not involve sin, like going bowling, gym, arcade, dinner, movies, etc. A Christian lifestyle is not a boring lifestyle; it's a safe and promising lifestyle. I want everyone to understand that you don't 'have to' go to church, you 'get to' go to church; you don't 'have to' praise God, you 'get to' praise God; you don't 'have to' come to God, you 'get to' come to God, these are privileges. Don't think that just because you have a lot of money and are doing financially well in your life that you are living a pleasing lifestyle to God. The bible says that God makes His sun rise on the evil and on the good, and sends rain on the just and on the unjust. **(Matthew 5:45)** It doesn't matter how rich you are; how much money you have; how popular you are or how much notoriety you have; you cannot buy your way into Heaven and when you die, you definitely can't take your riches with you. I'm not saying that if you are rich or have lots of money that you are a sinner, absolutely not! But what I am saying is don't think that money and power is an automatic ticket to Heaven. A lot of people spend their whole lifetime trying to become rich and famous instead of seeking God and living righteous. **"For what will it profit a man if he gains the whole world, and loses his own soul?" –Mark 8:36.** Your soul is the only thing that you own, everything else is just a temporary loan. Your soul is eternal. Death in the flesh is inevitable and you cannot escape it, but there is eternal life in Jesus. No other religion talks about saving you from the power of the grave. Buddha couldn't escape death, so how can he save you from death? Mohammad couldn't escape death, so how can he save you from death. Jesus is the only deity that conquered death and the power of the grave. Only He is able to give you eternal life in a glorious paradise, which is Heaven.

If there is anyone reading this book right now that is not saved or is living a lifestyle that is not compatible to a life of holiness and righteousness; if there's anyone reading this book right now who claims to be saved and redeemed, but just 'backslid'; if there's anyone reading this book right now who believes in God, but doesn't know him personally; if there's someone reading this book right now that is battling with any type of addiction or health issue; or if there's anyone reading this book right now who doesn't believe in Jesus or following a different religion other than Christianity, I want you to understand that God loves you. In **Matthew 24:37-44,** the bible talks about the Lord coming back as a thief in the night. If you believe that Jesus Christ is coming back, you have to know that there is no kind of way to predict when this time is going to be. Many people have tried to predict this day, but you see that we are still living and walking among the Earth. When the world ends, you are either going to Heaven or Hell, you make the choice. God has given every person in this world free will to choose their path. He lays the paths for you and shows you the right one to take, but the route you take is up to you. God is a gentleman and does not force anyone to turn to Him.

We were all born into sin and we all have sinned and fallen short of the glory of God. (**Romans 3:23**) I'm not perfect, no one is, but that is what the body of Christ (which is the church) is for. The church is to edify you and help you grow to be more Christ-like. It's not an overnight transformation and God knows that, but you have to decrease in your life so that He can increase in your life. **"The wages of sins is death, but the gifts of God is eternal life through Jesus Christ our Lord and Savior" -Romans 6:23.** Sin leads to eternal death, but the good news is that there is hope, because God loved us so much that while we were yet sinners, he sent his son, Jesus Christ to die for us. **(Romans 5:8)** When Jesus died on the cross he freed us from the enslavement of sin so that we may live for righteousness. **(1 Peter 2:24)** The Lord wants you to come to Him, He's calling you. How much money do you have? It doesn't matter, rich or poor. What color is your skin? It doesn't matter, black or white, brown or yellow. How well do you talk? It doesn't matter if you stutter or if you have great colloquialism. God has no respect of persons! **(Romans 2:11)** I don't want anyone to think that they have not sinned. The bible tells us that if we confess our sins that God will forgive us and cleanse us of those sins. **"If we say that we have no sin, we deceive ourselves, and the truth is not in us. If we confess our sins, he is faithful and just to forgive us our sins, and to cleanse us from all unrighteousness. If we say that we have not sinned, we make him a liar, and his word is not in us."- 1 John 1:8-10.** If you want to live righteous and holy today, all you have to do is confess with your mouth that Jesus is Lord and believe in your heart that God has raised Him from the dead. And you will be saved and share in the gift of salvation and eternal life in Heaven with Jesus Christ. **(Romans 10:9)**. The bible says that **"whosoever calls upon the name of the Lord shall be saved"** –**Romans 10:13.** All you have to do is call upon Him.

You can be saved today and all of your past sins will be washed away! **"Therefore, if anyone be in Christ, he is a new creation; <u>old things have passed away</u>; behold, all things have become new" – 2 Corinthians 5:17.** All you have to do is believe in your heart that God sent his son Jesus Christ to the earth to die for your sins; that Jesus Christ walked the earth, died, and rose on the third day; confess your sins; and ask God to come into your life and transform it, using you for His Kingdom work. I want everyone that is reading this book right now to just evaluate yourself. I don't care what your title is in the church, what kind of miracles you have performed, or how many people you have brought to Christ. I want you to evaluate your life right now. We all have made mistakes in our lives, I know that I have. The good thing about God is that He is forgiving, and that He is faithful and just, even when we are not faithful and we're not just. All you have to do is repent and you will be forgiven. The word <u>repent</u> means to turn away from, which means that you have to stop doing the sinful things that you are doing. That is true repentance. God wants us all to come into repentance because of his relentless, everlasting, and eternal love toward us. When I say evaluate, I mean look at your walk with God and see if you are lacking in **any** area of holiness or righteousness, or if you have been neglecting God in prayer, fasting, spreading the Gospel, etc. If you are serious about living for God, or reaching a new level of faith or glory, and want to be in the presence of the Lord forever, then repeat this prayer after me and mean it in your heart.

> **"God I come to You humble in the name of Jesus Christ and just recognize who You are in my life. I know that You are real and that You sent Your son Jesus Christ down to the earth to die for my sins and that He rose on the third day. I confess my sins to You. I am a sinner and I have lived a sinful life. I pray that You may come into my life and cleanse me and help me to live righteous. I love You Lord and I want You to come into my heart and come into my life and use me however you see fit. I have been hindering You from progressing in my life, and I am sorry for living for me, but now it is time to live for You. From this day forth, I pray that You may reign in my life and that I may do Your will, in Jesus name, Amen."**

Just that easy you are forgiven, just that easy you are given the inheritance of our Father, God.

If you said the prayer, you have been given a second chance at life, in spite of the horrible things that you have done in the past. Don't think about your previous sins, you are now a new creation (**2 Corinthians 5:17**). God has forgotten about your sins, so you also forget about them and start new. God said, **"I, even I, am He who blots out your transgressions for My own sake; and I will not remember your sins" – Isaiah 43:25.** Now it is time for you to progress and move forward. Don't focus on your past and all the wrong that you have done in your life, but focus on all the good that you can do now and all the people that you can redeem unto the Lord. The apostle Paul said in **Philippians 3:13 – "one thing I do is forgetting those things which are behind and reaching forward to those things which are ahead".** Now let everyone around you recognize a 'new you'. Let them see the difference in your life and recognize the Jesus that lives within you. Now that you are saved I want you to know a few things. First, the bible is meant to be food for daily use, not cake for special occasions. Don't neglect the bible, it is your guideline for living holy, don't let a day go by without reading some of it, this is vital to your walk with God. Jesus said, **"If you love Me, keep My commandments" –John 14:15.** In order to keep His commandments, you have to know His commandments, which come from reading His word. Second, sometimes God doesn't change your situation because he's trying to change your heart. God knows what you can handle, but he loves to see you overcome test and trials because it strengthens your faith in Him, so don't give up. Don't worry, the bible says, **"No temptation has overtaken you except such as is common to man; but God *is* faithful, who will not allow you to be tempted beyond what you are able, but with the temptation will also make the way of escape, that you may be able to bear it" -1 Corinthians 10:13.** God will not put you in a situation that you can't handle, and always provides a way out of it if it gets too much for you. A lot of times God wants to deal with your heart more than your sin. Third, until God opens the next door, praise him in the hallway in advance. Faith is what pleases God and He rewards those that diligently seek after him. **(Hebrews 11:6)**

Don't begin to doubt God because you are experiencing a storm in your life, you must make it through the storm to see the rainbow. The race is not given to the swift or to the strong (**Ecclesiastes 9:11**), but to him who endures to the end. So continuously praise God in spite of your situation. Lastly, what if you woke up today with only the things that you thanked God for yesterday? For some people this can be a great thing, while for some people they might only wake up with their life, if even that. You have to give God thanks and praise for everything that happens in your life, He is the reason for it. (**Psalms 136:1**) I thank God every morning I wake up, for things that I used to have, things that I currently have, and things that I will have. That's faith, thanking Him in advance. Don't take for granted what God has given you, because just as easy as you attained it, the same way He can take it away. So understand who God is and the impact that He has on the things in your life. If you have never trusted in God before, give Him a try. You gave sin a chance, so give God a chance. I am a witness that He will show himself faithful. **"Oh, taste and see that the Lord is good" –Psalms 34:8.**

CLOSING

I would like to thank everyone that read this book and I pray that you received something from it. Whether salvation if you were not saved or rededication if you were saved at one time but fell from grace. If you were already saved and living a holy and righteous lifestyle, I hope you received some good advice. I also just want to again thank my wife, Nicole, for continuously being in my corner and supporting me throughout my witnessing quest and writing this book. I want to thank my pastors, Pastor Reginald and Delphine Glenn for encouraging me and continuously imparting knowledge into me. I really want to thank my brother in Christ, Minister Dorian Harvey for being my faithful partner while out ministering. He was definitely a helpful inspiration to me while we were out there ministering the Gospel and I honestly don't think that I could have completed this quest without him. Thanks Dorian for your faithfulness and obedience to the Holy Spirit. I also want to recognize all of my family and friends that have supported me, thank you all! I wish that you all will continue to pray for me and all the other Christians all the frontline of defending the Gospel. To God be the glory! Amen!

AFTERWORD

Earlier in the year of 2014, Pastor Reggie prophesied over me and told me that a backlash from the devil was going to take place. He said that the devil was mad because of my soul winning quest. He told me that there would be no way around it and that I would have to endure and go through it. So, I began to prepare for it by praying and fasting more often. Well in October 2014, I endured a major backlash from the devil on my job. In November 2014, Pastor Reggie prophesied over me again not even knowing what was going on. He told me that what was going on at my job was a conspiracy set up by the devil, and that I had to continue to trust in God. If I haven't prepared for this attack, it would have caught me off guard and hit me hard. One scripture that I held onto was **James 1:12 – "Blessed is the man who endures temptation; for when he has been approved, he will receive the crown of life which the Lord has promised to those who love Him."** I go into great detail about this situation on my job and explain everything and expose all secrets and conspiracies in my upcoming book. This was something big and a huge blow to me and my family, but "For God's glory, I will do anything, or go through anything." Remember that God's children will ALWAYS be victorious!!!

33309552R00071

Made in the USA
Middletown, DE
08 July 2016